Building Bright
Futures

Neuro Therapy Toolkit

JENNY CLUNING

First published by Busybird Publishing 2020

ISBN: 978-1-922465-37-5 (paperback)

Cover Image: Sandra Garvey
Layout and typesetting: Busybird Publishing

Busybird Publishing
2/118 Para Road
Montmorency, Victoria
Australia 3094

Dedication

The encouragement and inspiration I have constantly received from my devoted husband Anthony has ensured that I have continued to develop professionally.

To my precious children, Mark, Nick and Adam, for being great role models in their own right, for persistence and for resilience.

To Estie Bav, author of the book *Growing Beautiful Teeth*, for inspiring me and giving me the courage and confidence to write this book.

Lastly, to my dear friends Pamela Ashby, Cranial Sacral and Movement Therapist, Glynis Brummer from Smart Learning Solutions in Auckland NZ, and Ian McGowan from the Movement and Learning Centre in Scotland, for their friendship, learning and ongoing support along the journey.

BUILDING BRIGHT FUTURES
Neuro Therapy Toolkit

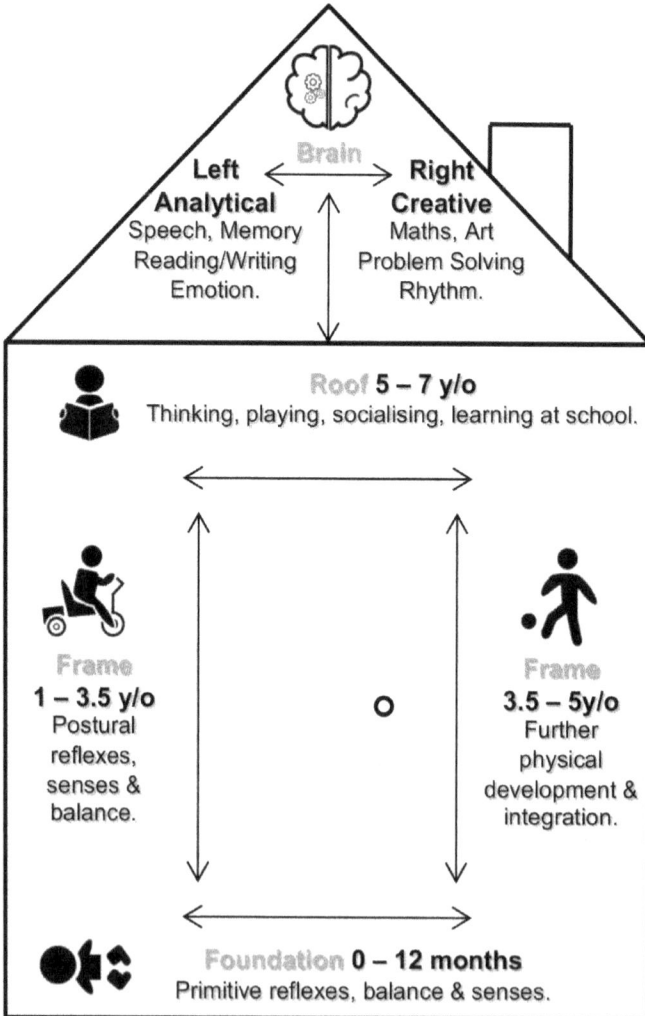

Brain

Left Analytical
Speech, Memory
Reading/Writing
Emotion.

← →

Right Creative
Maths, Art
Problem Solving
Rhythm.

Roof 5 – 7 y/o
Thinking, playing, socialising, learning at school.

Frame
1 – 3.5 y/o
Postural
reflexes,
senses &
balance.

Frame
3.5 – 5y/o
Further
physical
development &
integration.

Foundation 0 – 12 months
Primitive reflexes, balance & senses.

Contents

Foreword   i

Special Note   v

Introduction   vii

1. The Journey   1

Foundation: 0 – 12 Months   **11**

2. Understanding Early Development   13

3. Understanding Primitive Reflexes   31

Frame: 1 – 3.5 years old / 3.5 to 5 years old   **39**

4. Understanding Postural Reflexes   41

5. Wired Through Movement   47

6. Discover the Senses   59

Roof: 5 – 7 years old   **73**

7. The Plastic Brain   75

8. School Readiness Framework   83

Neuro Therapy Tool Kit   **91**

9. Ultimate Neuro Therapies   93

10. Additional Neurological Support   105

Bright Future Testimonials   **121**

Stories and Testimonials   123

About the Author   133

Acknowledgements   139

Foreword

I first met Jenny Cluning in 2013 whilst delivering a training course on Bilateral Integration Movement in Melbourne, Victoria. Over subsequent years, I got to know her as a friend and a loving mother to her family, including her two youngest sons, Adam and Nick, who have required on-going support from a young age and interventions to release their potential and help them be the best they can be.

I have over 40 years of professional experience in physical education, psychology, neuro-developmental and movement therapy, and child development in a range of settings. Since 2004 I have worked in private practice in Scotland with children and adolescents with learning and behavioural difficulties. Parents whose children I have worked with have generally shown great commitment to helping their children, none more so than Jenny supported by her husband Anthony.

Hers is a remarkable story of love, devotion, determination and perseverance to find solutions to her boys' difficulties. Like many parents, Jenny accessed available medical and educational support from public sector professionals, but then went on a quest to find other support and interventions which could add further value for her boys. Over years of unswerving and on-going support for her boys (including eldest son Mark), Jenny has acquired a significant body of knowledge, experience, and wisdom from her studies and training and from working with her own children and those of other families.

The interventions chosen for her children were selected on the basis of what might work to improve their status. These programmes may not be evidence based from a strict scientific point of view but from experiences of other practitioners have been shown to have positive outcomes. They were all non-invasive, home-based programmes and highly unlikely to do any harm.

If you are a parent, carer, teacher or practitioner working with children or adolescents who need additional support you should read this book. Jenny's story will provide hope that there is more we can do to help our children and adolescents achieve more than may be thought possible. This book is a useful starting point for further exploration, study and training.

Since the first Bilateral Integration Movement Training Course in Melbourne in 2013, I have been fortunate to personally witness the development of Adam and Nick over the next five years through subsequent training courses and continued contact with Jenny. The progress the boys have made in that time is remarkable, with each making great advances in life skills, sports and academics. This is on-going at the time of writing and their story is not yet complete. I have no hesitation in saying this has been life changing for them — if their initial developmental status had been accepted as a given, there would have been potentially significantly poorer life outcomes than is now the case. Isn't that something worth shouting about and sharing with others? From the testimonials from parents included in the book (and from those I have worked with over the last 16 years) the answer to that question is a resounding YES!

This book provides personal insights from the author and opens doors to possibilities and opportunities that many who read this may not have been aware of. As such I highly recommend it to you, and trust that you will be both uplifted by the story and much enlightened by the experience of reading it.

– Ian McGowan

Special Note

OAM for service to education as a teacher and administrator of specialist schools.

As an experienced educator of children with special needs, I have found parents benefit in many ways from sharing their concerns with others. We all like to find solutions to our challenges. We ask friends for advice, professionals for guidance, and often spend sleepless nights searching for ideas.

Jenny Cluning has gathered, collected, organised, researched and carefully written this book to help, guide, inspire and help every one of us who has ever had that sleepless night.

Thank-you, Jenny, for embarking on the challenge of writing a book to help others by sharing your experiences and knowledge with others.

– Helen Hatherly

Introduction

For many years, a goal of mine has been to write a book that shares and passes on my knowledge and experience in childhood development to teachers and parents/carers in the community. I have acquired this wisdom through attending many training courses and presenting workshops to both parents/carers and educators in the Move to Learn program and various information sessions.

Over the years I have worked with both my own children and with other parents and their children. This has provided me with a unique insight into the needs of children, their parents, and the support they both require to achieve a high level of life skills and release potential.

This book outlines the journey I have been through, gives a brief overview of early childhood development, major milestones from birth to five years, and some factors that may affect or interfere with development. Also included is an overview of the connections between the brain and movement, followed by primitive and postural reflexes, the vestibular system and the five senses. A description of neuroplasticity is outlined, and information is provided on neuro-therapies that may assist with improving motor control, learning, behaviour, focus and concentration, even sports performance.

Finally, there are additional neurological supports, followed by several stories and testimonials giving a brief account of success and progress some of my clients have achieved.

1

The Journey

In 2008, my husband and I embarked on a pathway to find solutions to help our five-year-old son, who was diagnosed with a severe language disorder, mild autism and an intellectual impairment.

After seeing positive results through hard work and commitment to the programs, my husband and I thought our seven-year-old son may also benefit from both the auditory and development movement therapy programs. It is worth noting these neuro-therapies were supported by various psychologists, speech therapists and tutors.

Here is a brief case history of both boys, showing the challenges they faced and their amazing improvements.

Adam's Story
A boy with mild autism, severe language delay and intellectual impairment.

Adam's development in-utero was relatively normal, however, there are two factors worth sharing. The first is that his movement inside the womb was often quite minimal and during the pregnancy I had four foetal monitors to measure his heart rate and rhythm.

Secondly, I suffered a bacterial sinus infection at approximately 34 weeks where I experienced high fevers and felt generally unwell for two weeks. Given the nature of the infection I was prescribed antibiotics which helped dramatically. However, during a regular check up with my obstetrician at approximately 36 weeks, it was noted Adam hadn't grown much over the last fortnight.

My obstetrician organised an ultrasound, which showed there was low amniotic fluid surrounding him. This low amniotic fluid may have been a result of the high fevers from the bacterial infection and thus affected his growth and development during this time. Following this ultrasound, I was monitored regularly by my obstetrician and tried to rest as much as possible.

During my next pre-natal appointment, at approximately 38 weeks, my obstetrician noted an improvement in Adam's growth and the results of another ultrasound showed my amniotic fluid had increased to normal levels.

Adam is my third child and arrived very quickly into the world in approximately 35 minutes, naturally and without any birth intervention. He was quite unsettled during the 48 hours post birth, finding it difficult to latch onto the breast when feeding and refusing to take any expressed milk from a cup.

The midwife on duty at the time, who was trying to feed Adam expressed milk from a cup asked, "Has someone checked to see if he has a tongue-tie? A baby with a tongue-tie may find it difficult to latch onto the breast and stay latched on."

The next morning my obstetrician came in, and from both the midwife's notes and my comments on how he was struggling to feed, checked Adam for a tongue-tie. Following an examination of Adam's mouth, my obstetrician noted this was definitely the case and recommended it be released through a procedure where the piece of skin under the tongue (frenulum) is snipped.

Following this minor procedure, it didn't take long for Adam to latch onto the breast, feed and be generally much more settled.

From three months to two years of age, Adam suffered ear infections and chronic tonsillitis approximately every three to four months. As a result of many upper respiratory illnesses with high fevers, he didn't spend enough time on the floor moving his body and skipped crawling on all fours. This may have contributed to a significant delay in his language and motor skills. At age two, Adam was only using two-word phrases and found it difficult to jump with two feet and catch a ball with two hands.

After Adam's second birthday he had an operation to remove his tonsils and adenoids. On day five post-surgery, Adam suffered a post-op bleed at home. He was re-admitted to hospital where the ear, nose and throat surgeon cauterised his throat to stop the bleeding. Adam spent a further two nights in hospital recovering and learning how to swallow.

Following his recovery Adam's language started to slowly pick up, and he was beginning to say four to five-word phrases — e.g. 'I want to go in water' — and show more confidence in his motor skills.

Not long after his fourth birthday Adam started to develop behavioural problems. He lost interest in drawing, showed high levels of frustration and felt overwhelmed with the world around him.

His language skills suddenly dropped to mostly one-word utterances, and his speech became unclear. He began to play with his toys closely and displayed little interest in playing with his brothers anymore.

Adam seemed to be in his own world, had poor eye contact, delayed speech and language, as well as poor motor coordination and emotional regulation.

The year before he started school, my husband and I sought help from a professional therapy centre in Melbourne, to assist with Adam's neurodevelopmental delay (NDD). This delay was picked up by Adam's kindergarten teacher, and was also of some concern to my husband and I.

Adam began intensive in-clinic sound therapy, which was two hours a day, five days a week over a three-week period. After each intensive block of listening, Adam had a home program, completed over eight weeks, which consisted of 45 minutes a day, five days a week.

Following the sound therapy, Adam went through a series of reflex integration floor movements and bean bag exercises to assist his partially retained primitive reflexes, underdeveloped postural reflexes and sensory system.

Through hard work, commitment and perseverance on a daily basis, through the sound and movement programs Adam made amazing positive changes which have helped him to shine bright. Below are some observations noted from my husband, myself, the Leaping Lizards instructor (a weekly activity group Adam attended — more information can be found on pg. 56) and his Kindergarten teaching staff.

Parent Observations

After only a few months, Adam showed improvements in his eye contact, concentration and speech and language. He was beginning to show signs of sharing with his brothers at home and playing dress up games.

Adam appeared to be more spontaneous with his greetings, saying both hello and goodbye to family and friends, but still required frequent prompting. My husband and I also noticed a huge improvement in his motor skills, which was evident when catching a ball, running, jumping and climbing.

Leaping Lizards Instructor Observations

"Adam has shown great improvement in his concentration and he is also able to listen to and follow instructions with more focus and eye contact. He also is now able to understand concepts of 'under', 'on', 'in' and 'next to'. Adam's balance and coordination have greatly improved, which could be seen when he was using the climbing equipment and when sitting on the floor in a group activity."

Observations from Kindergarten Teaching Staff

"We are noticing that Adam is becoming a lot more verbal and asking for help. He is more interested in interacting and engaging with other children even though he found it difficult to put words and sentences together. He now really enjoys participating in dancing and his gross and fine motor skills have made significant changes. He is able to cut with scissors whilst doing an activity and he is able to sit and concentrate on the floor for longer periods."

Where he is now

Today, as an 18-year-old in his final year at school, Adam excels in swimming, dancing, and enjoys learning to sing and play the piano. He still finds reading and expressing his thoughts challenging but has shown great maturity when socially engaging in sporting and musical settings as well as at family functions.

Adam has won various swimming awards in the multiclass category at both Regional and State championship level. In 2018 Adam achieved second place in backstroke at Regional level and went on to compete at State level where he achieved third place.

The following year Adam swam in the Regional championships, this time in freestyle, breaststroke and backstroke. He won first place in the freestyle and backstroke and second place in the breaststroke. Again, Adam went on to compete at State level, where he competed in backstroke and freestyle, where he went one better to achieve second place in backstroke and fourth place in the freestyle.

These neuro-therapy programs have not taken away his mild autism, severe language disorder and mild intellectual impairment, but hard work and commitment to these programs have had an enormous impact in helping him shine bright and achieve success.

Nick's Story
A boy with mild intellectual impairment

Nick's development in-utero was normal and he was born without any birth intervention. As a baby he was quite settled when feeding and sleeping, and during the first six months post-birth Nick had lots of time on the floor learning to move his body and explore the world. He progressed through the developmental stages, although he skipped commando crawling on his stomach and only crawled on all fours for approximately four weeks.

Once Nick was able to sit on the floor by himself, he was content and happy to play with his toys rather than crawl on all fours. His older brother, Mark, loved to play with Nick and enjoyed collecting his toys and balls for him.

At six months Nick started having ear infections approximately every three months, needing antibiotics and suffering extremely high fevers each time.

Around 15 months old Nick started getting tonsillitis, which returned every four months until he was three years old. Each time he suffered a bought of tonsillitis he developed high fevers and generally felt lethargic and unwell. During this time Nick missed out on a lot of opportunities to develop his gross motor skills and postural reflexes. As a result, his language and auditory processing was delayed so he typically uttered only three to four words at a time. He also had very enlarged tonsils and snored at night which greatly interrupted his sleep.

At three and a half, Nick's tonsils and adenoids were removed. Within a couple of months of the surgery his speech doubled, and he was saying eight-word phrases.

Nick was a confident boy who always socialised and interacted with other children and his teachers in kindergarten well. When Nick was five, he was in four-year-old kindergarten and his teacher noticed he was showing signs of delay in his language. She also noted that Nick appeared to find jigsaw puzzles challenging, and had poor concentration, attention, auditory processing, fine motor and memory skills.

His teacher suggested that Nick might benefit from speech therapy, which could potentially help his auditory processing, memory and concentration skills.

Nick attended weekly speech therapy sessions for approximately two years from the age of five to seven. During these sessions Nick did lots of activities with the therapist, but still appeared to have difficulty retaining and remembering what he had learnt.

During Nick's prep year, his teacher, who was so supportive, suggested he may benefit from some support in the classroom, especially heading into grade one. The school arranged for a psychologist from the Catholic Education Office to conduct a full assessment. From this assessment Nick was diagnosed with a mild intellectual impairment, which, as a mother, was initially difficult to process and understand.

Nick headed into grade one a happy and confident boy with an Individual Learning Plan from the teacher, as well as integration aide support. This support in the classroom was integral for Nick allowing to learn with his peers.

When Nick's younger brother, Adam, was halfway through his sound therapy and movement program, my husband and I realised Nick may benefit from both the sound and developmental movement programs, too.

At age seven Nick went through a course of intense sound therapy, followed by an eight-week program in between the intensive blocks. After the sound therapy program, Nick went through a series of primitive reflex and balance movement exercises from various therapies. These therapies — Extra Lesson, Rhythmic Movement, INPP, Move to Learn and Bilateral Integration — are detailed further in Chapter 9.

Below is an outline of improvements my husband and I and teachers noted.

Parent Observations

After one week of intensive sound therapy, Nick appeared to enjoy reading more. There was a slight improvement in the way he followed text with his eyes, and he was more confident when trying new words.

At the end of the second week, Nick showed great enjoyment and confidence every time he read out aloud. He also appeared to show improvement in his memory, remembering new words from previous books. Nick's concentration grew and he showed improvement in spatial awareness, writing, drawing and his ability to complete puzzles.

Nick kept improving every week. His memory recall showed improvement and he would remember which football teams had played and who won or lost. He was able to follow two-step instructions at home and would also remember if he had to bring something different to school the next day. Nick's writing was more legible and his gross motor skills, which had always been quite sound, were even stronger.

There was a huge improvement in his balance, and he was able to sit and concentrate in the classroom for longer periods and was less fatigued after doing sporting activities. In particular, it was noted that his hand-eye coordination when playing sport was excellent.

School/Teachers Observations

"He appears to be enjoying reading more and wants to attempt more than one book when reading out loud by himself. There is a slight improvement in the way he is following text with his eyes, remembering a word he has read from a previous reader and reading more fluently.

Before starting the sound therapy, he was reading books with basic text, generally at Level One. After three weeks of sound therapy his reading was re-tested under the PM Benchmark and this showed that he was now reading at Level Five with 95 per cent accuracy and 100 per cent comprehension.

He is showing improved confidence and concentration when reading and also when doing jigsaw puzzles, writing and drawing.

His handwriting is continuing to improve, as is his focus and concentration as he is able to sit for longer periods and work independently. One area that improved dramatically was his spelling.

Before starting the sound therapy and movement exercises, he could only manage five spelling words with minimal accuracy. After six weeks of therapy he could comfortably and accurately do ten basic spelling words. His memory and recall improved dramatically, and he is much more aware when reading out loud of his mistakes.

Two other areas that showed improvement were both his spelling and writing. He was now able to spell 15–20 three letter words accurately and he displayed a significant improvement in his balance and hand-eye coordination."

Later high school years to now

Nick completed year eleven and twelve through a hands-on education program which had a sporting focus. This was a perfect program for Nick as his passion for basketball allowed him to gain experience through volunteer work within the basketball industry as well as to further develop his coaching skills. At the completion of year twelve he attained Certificate II and Certificate III in Sport and Recreation with the assistance of a weekly tutor. Through Nick's hard work and commitment in his final two years of school he was presented with the overall class award and also received an award recognising his outstanding contribution towards Basketball Victoria.

Now, in 2020, as a young adult, Nick's passion for basketball has truly reached another level both on and off the court. Off the court his communication, ability to coach children and pass on his passion and knowledge of the game has become some of his greatest strengths. On the court his leadership ability, focus, concentration and ability to listen to coaches' instructions wouldn't be where it is if all of us hadn't committed to the movement and listening programs over many years, especially during his early teenage years. Nick was also the proud winner of the 2019 Basketball Athlete of the Year with an Intellectual Disability award from Basketball Victoria.

Throughout this long journey, it has been wonderful to witness Adam and Nick's older brother, Mark, provide support and encouragement by being a great role model and caring brother.

Personally, I have learnt that sometimes one program isn't enough and that you may need to search through many programs to find one that is suitable, engaging and works for your child. My many years of being involved in neuro-therapy interventions has taught me that individuals can also improve their sports performance by fine tuning their sensory system through commitment and perseverance.

Working with my own children has provided me with a unique insight into the needs of children, their parents and the support required to unlock their brightest future and the special talent that is in everyone. With daily commitment and patience, there are endless possibilities.

FOUNDATION
0 – 12 MONTHS

Primitive reflexes, balance & senses.

2

Understanding Early Development

Development In-utero

Development in-utero occurs over nine months or 38 to 40 weeks and is when the baby initially gains sensory input. During this time the baby goes through amazing changes that prepare them for the outside sensory world. There are three stages of development in-utero in which the baby develops their sensory system and learns about the world around them: germinal, embryonic and foetal.

Germinal Stage

This first stage of pre-natal development takes place over a two-week period from the beginning of conception. During this 14-day phase, the fertilised cell rapidly divides and multiplies, by which the cells become more specialised and form different parts of the body and organs to make the embryo ready for the next stage. The uniqueness of these multiple cells also creates the placenta, umbilical cord and amniotic fluid to support further growth and development.

Embryonic Stage

The embryonic stage is from two to eight weeks of pregnancy and is when the multicellular structure implants itself into the wall of the uterus.

During this time the placenta grows and forms blood vessels so it can attach to the wall of the uterus. The placenta delivers nutrients and oxygen to the foetus as well as assisting with eliminating waste products from the blood. At seven to eight weeks the first sense to develop is touch, with taste emerging at around eight weeks.

Foetal Stage

This last stage of pre-natal development is the longest of the three. It begins around nine weeks and lasts until birth. The sense of touch continues to develop and at eleven to twelve weeks in-utero the foetus will start to make small movements. These first small and slight movements are the start of the foetus gaining an understanding the world around them.

Primitive reflexes start to emerge between 9 and 12 weeks. By 13 to 15 weeks the baby's tastebuds have further developed and the foods the expectant mum eats can flavour the amniotic fluid.

At around 16 weeks the fingers and toes of the baby are fully developed. It is also around this time hearing begins to develop.

Between 16 and 28 weeks, the baby's neural connections increase, their size and weight double, as well as becoming more coordinated when moving their limbs and body.

From approximately 30 to 32 weeks the baby's growth slows down, but they will continue to gain weight and length up until birth.

Development Post-birth

A child goes through many milestones after they are born, with some of the major developmental ones being:

- Physical Development
  - » Gross Motor
  - » Fine Motor
- Speech and Language
- Intellectual
- Emotional

Physical Development

Gross Motor

During the first 12 months the baby gains basic gross motor skills by playing and learning to move their body on the floor. This period of floor movement is critical as it lays the foundations for later development and lifelong learning.

Before an infant can learn to sit up, they must gain control over the head, shoulders, chest and trunk. Lots of time on the tummy helps the infant develop strength in this region of their body. Following this the child must be able to hold their head up while lying on their tummy and roll from their front to their back before they can sit up.

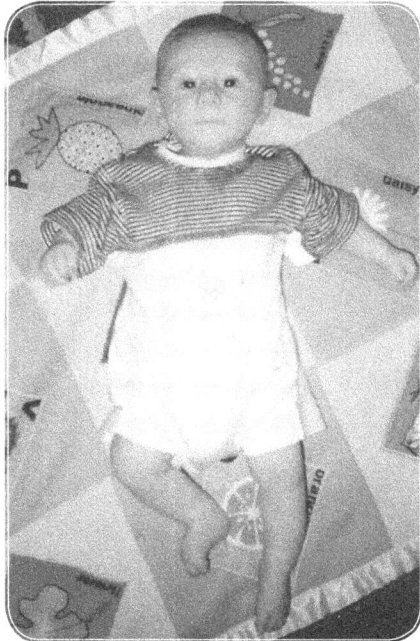

Once an infant has passed these milestones, they will have more control over their legs which will help them progress through the next important sequences of crawling on hands and knees, walking and running.

Typically, after a child's first birthday they are able to stand up, walk alone and stand on tip toe. They can also climb stairs unassisted, and often enjoy climbing on furniture as well as playing at the park. Activities in the garden, such as helping mum, dad or grandparents are also enjoyed.

Playing at the park and on other equipment at home can further develop the balance system and postural reflexes. Closer to their second birthday the child can learn the motion of kicking a ball and is able to carry large toys and objects while walking.

Between the ages of two and three, a child's gross motor skills have further developed, and they should be able to jump, climb stairs with two feet and throw a ball with two hands. When running the child will look quite awkward in their motion. They should be able to ride a toy trike, pushing their feet along the ground to move themselves forward.

After the age of three a child becomes more coordinated. They will begin to be able to hop like a bunny rabbit and should be able to pedal and steer a bike with training wheels. They should be able to catch a ball with two hands and throw an object with one hand in an underarm motion.

The child should be able to walk down steps with two feet on each step, and when walking their arms will swing freely and naturally by their sides.

At the age of four to five, a child should be able to alternate their feet when walking up and down stairs. Their balance system has developed further, which can be seen when skipping, hopping on one foot or riding a bike without training wheels in a rapid and smooth motion.

Fine Motor

Fine motor skills begin to develop once inborn primitive reflexes have been modified and a child starts to use their upper body to reach and grasp for different objects, as well as passing an item, such as a cube, from one hand to the other. Between six and twelve months, the pincer grip starts to develop, and the infant begins to move and observe various objects as it crawls around. The infant can sit on the floor playing and placing different shaped objects into a container.

Typically, between the ages of 12 months and 2 years a child will enjoy scribbling with large crayons, painting and independently turning the pages of a book. When playing with toys, the developing child will be able to construct a tower of at least two blocks, sometimes up to four.

In the next phase of development between the ages of two and three, the toddler's fine motor control becomes more refined. They become more skilled at feeding themselves with a spoon and have more control with their mouth when drinking from a cup using a straw. Fine motor control in the hands and fingers become more proficient as the toddler is able to turn knobs on doors and toys and demonstrate the beginnings of washing their hands by themselves. They also enjoy opening cupboards, drawers and boxes, and can build a tower of at least three to four blocks, sometimes up to six.

Between the ages of three and four, a child's fine motor control further increases. Their construction ability usually

includes building a tower of at least eight blocks. The child has also gained further control when drinking from a cup and may enjoy cutting small pieces of paper, which assists in the further development of their fine motor control. When using crayons or pencils they have gone from scribbling to being able to draw a circle and a cross.

Following on from this, fine motor skills between the ages of four and five have become more established. The child can independently eat with a fork and spoon and are more accurate and able to cut longer pieces of paper when using scissors. Threading beads of different shapes and sizes is an activity that produces lots of enjoyment, as does seeing what happens when items or liquid are poured from containers. The child can now typically draw a circle, a square and a person with two to four body parts.

Heading to school, a child aged five to seven should be able to copy a triangle, as well as other geometric patterns plus a person with a whole body. They can trace around their hand using a pencil or crayon, copy some capital letters and cut along lines.

During this stage of development, a child's preferred or dominant hand usually becomes clear.

The picture below depicts an approximate age for basic prewriting shapes relating to Fine Motor control.

Basic Pre-Writing Skills Shapes

1–2 years	2–3 years	3–4 years	4–5 years	5–6 years	6–7 years (a, b, c)(1, 2, 3)
Scribbles	Horizontal and vertical lines	Copies a circle	Copies a square and cross	Copies a triangle	Cross midlines and form letters, numbers

Speech and Language

For the first few months after birth, the baby typically makes noises such as crying and coughing, plus little sounds while breathing.

At some stage between one and three months, the baby starts to make cooing noises such as "oohh" and "ah". It is through this cooing control that the muscles required to talk are developed.

Following this, approximately between the ages of two and eight months, the baby likes to play and experiment with different sounds beginning with the vowels, 'a, e, i, o, u'.

These sounds are very playful and if parents and family members provide lots of interaction during this stage, the baby will be encouraged to use consonant sounds.

Vocal play continues with babbling and recurring syllables such as "a-la-la", which can often appear like their own language. From approximately eight months up to one year, the baby will babble less and will begin to produce sounds like "da-da" and "ma-ma" — however, the babbling will continue up until the child's second birthday.

In an attempt to produce their first word, the infant will start to use sounds like "fla", "ma", and "ba". Usually around a child's first birthday or the onset of walking, they will say their first word, can understand approximately 20 words and say three to eight single words such as "ball", "mama", "milk".

From one to two years, a child's speech and language increases. They become almost like a parrot, listening carefully to the tone of voice and trying to repeat the sounds they have just heard. A child will also begin to use hand gestures once they are using two words and particularly enjoy saying "no" and "mine" frequently.

Continuing on, between the ages of two and three a typically developing child will know approximately 50 words and speak in sentences with three to four words. They enjoy asking lots of questions all the time and continually ask "why" to gain more information about the world around them. Singing and repeating nursery rhymes can be a fun and enjoyable experience to assist with continuing to develop speech and language.

At around four to five, a child's grammar becomes more complex, using sentences with around five or more words. For example, they might say, "Mummy cooks in the kitchen".

Intellectual Development

Intellectual development begins early after birth, with the infant learning about the world around them through their senses and the environment they live in.

In 1936 the psychologist Jean Piaget developed the theory that there are four stages of cognitive (intellectual) development. The first two stages are Sensorimotor (infancy), which typically happens between birth and two years, and Pre-operational (toddler and early childhood) which occurs approximately between the ages of two and seven.

Sensorimotor stage – birth to two years

During this stage of intellectual development, the infant is in a period of rapid growth. Through lots of floor time, physical movement and sensory experiences the infant learns about their body, how it works, and their surroundings.

With lots of learning and development opportunities in the motor milestones, such as rolling, sitting, crawling and walking, an infant will gain knowledge and develop a rich network of neurons, allowing for memory to start developing from approximately seven months old. The important foundational level for higher level thinking, language and social engagement is laid at this age and in this way.

Pre-operational stage — Two to Seven years

Around two years of age, a child's language appears and increases rapidly. They have difficulty with logic and understanding, but memory and imagination start to become more developed. The child may make up imaginary friends and enjoy pretend play through dressing up as one of their favourite characters.

Emotional Development

The development of emotional skills starts to appear very early on. Shortly after birth the baby shows signs of emotional development through distress, discomfort, anger, fear and joy.

During the first few months, the baby communicates their basic needs such as hunger, tiredness, hot, cold, pain or loneliness by crying.

As these needs are met the baby forms an emotional bond with their caregiver. This strong emotional bond forms an attachment which ultimately helps the infant build trust in others in future relationships.

In the first six months an infant does not feel love and affection because they are totally reliant on their carer. It is sometime within the second half of the first year that babies start to show affection towards their parents by kissing and hugging.

Between one and three months of age the baby begins to gently smile if they feel happy and will cry when they feel uncomfortable. Towards the end of the third month the baby's smile becomes more noticeable.

At around five months the baby starts to display more emotion. For example, they may show signs of being scared of strangers, they may arch their back in sheer anger, spit out food that is not liked and smile more often.

Between seven and twelve months old anger and fear increase, and the baby may also show signs of being more anxious of strangers.

After the first birthday and as a toddler starts to say their first words, they begin to want more control by saying "no" and really stamping their authority. They don't like sharing and become very possessive of their toys.

Somewhere between the ages of three and seven a child begins to control their emotions while becoming more independent. Emotions such as shame, embarrassment and pride begin to take shape, as does a rise in self-esteem. During this time when strongly felt emotions can take over, a child needs love, help and support from their caregiver to understand appropriate behaviour to learn how to control their own emotions and understand others.

Underlying Factors Affecting Development

To a large extent the baby's health depends on genetics and the health and lifestyle of their parents before and during conception.

An individual's genes are the basic physical and functional molecular unit and are inherited from parents. They determine personality, height, hair, eyes and skin colour.

Smoking, excessive alcohol, body temperatures over 39 degrees, viral infections, and poor diet during pregnancy may affect the developing foetus and the efficiency of the placenta.

There can be many other factors affecting childhood development and milestones. When looking at the table on page 27, it can be important to remember it is not just one or two things that may interfere or affect a child's development but a cluster of factors, usually more than three, from various areas and environmental situations.

Below are two case examples, Child A and Child B, that show a cluster of circumstances that may have contributed to a delay in development.

Child A – aged five
at the time of investigating therapy interventions

1. Mum suffered a viral infection with a high fever over 39 degrees during pregnancy
2. There was a placenta insufficiency – 'low lying fluid'
3. Not a lot of in-utero movement
4. Precipitate Labour – (first and second stage of labour combined – usually under two hours – and the baby was born without needing to push)
5. From two months to two years of age, Child A had recurrent ear, nose and throat infections, before having tonsils and adenoids removed
6. Floor movements on the floor for Child A was restricted in the first six months.
   a. Skipped crawling on all fours, and
   b. Went straight to walking at approximately 12 months

Child B – aged seven
at the time of investigating therapy interventions

1. Child B had interrupted movement on the floor
   a. Skipped commando crawling;
   b. Was propped up by pillows before having the core strength to hold body upright in this position naturally; and
   c. Crawled on all fours for only a short time, approximately four to six weeks
2. Child B had recurrent ear nose and throat infections with very high fevers from 12 months to three and half years of age
3. Tonsils and adenoids removed at age three and a half

As you can see, both Child A and Child B encountered a different cluster of challenges during their developmental stages.

However, neuro-therapy interventions allowed both to shine so brightly in their everyday life skills and future.

There are many underlying factors that could contribute to challenges a person may sustain in areas such as motor development, learning and social engagement.

When looking behind the symptoms of an individual's difficulties or challenges we can see there is a delay in the neurological system.

This interruption can also be referred to as Neurodevelopment Delay (NDD).

Neurodevelopment Delay (NDD)

When looking at NDD we need to understand that every person is born with a set of primitive reflexes, also known as survival reflexes.

If these primitive reflexes aren't fully integrated during infancy, control of voluntary, skilled and complex motor movements may be affected.

They may also interfere with the normal stages of motor development, visual functioning, hand-eye coordination and perceptual skills.

As a result, individuals may suffer from social and emotional challenges, hyperactivity and hypersensitivity, as well as poor motor control, concentration and short-term memory.

Author, lecturer and International Director of The Institute for Neuro-Physiological Psychology, Sally Goddard-Blythe, describes NDD as: "The continued presence of a cluster of primitive reflexes beyond the first six months of post-natal life, with or without, absence of under-developed postural reflexes beyond three and a half years of age."

Four areas that may be worth considering as possible causes of NDD can be categorised under the umbrella of Pregnancy, Birth, Newborn disorders and Early Childhood.

Below is a diagram of these four categories with highlighted areas showing a cluster of factors.

Pregnancy	Birth		Early Childhood
• Threatened miscarriage	• **Long or precipitate labour**	• Birth weight	• **Illnesses in early childhood**
• Influenza or infection at specific stages	• Foetal distress	• Inborn errors of metabolism	• Febrile convulsion
• Toxaemia	• Prematurity	• Low apgar score	• **Restricted movement in the first months**
• Poorly controlled diabetes	• Breach presentation		• **History of recurrent ear, nose and throat infections**
• **Placental insufficiency**	• Caesarean section, high forceps delivery, ventouse extraction		
• **Reduced amniotic fluid**			
• Poor nutrition			

If a parent/carer or teacher is concerned about a child's development at any stage, it is important to seek advice from a professional such as a paediatrician, psychologist, occupational or speech therapist.

From my personal experience I have found it helpful to look at various neuro-therapies which are designed to look behind the symptoms and challenges an individual may be encountering. When looking over the early years, milestones and development of a child, we can see early movement plays a crucial role in not only physical growth, but also speech, language, intellectual and emotional development.

Chapter Resources

DEVELOPMENT IN-UTERO

Pre-natal Development, Lumen Boundless Psychology, https://courses. lumenlearning.com/boundless-psychology/chapter/prenatal-development/.

The secret world of the unborn – how your baby's senses develop in the womb, BabySense, https://www.babysense.com/advice-and-tips/the-secret-world-of-the-unborn-how-your-babys-senses-develop-in-the-womb/.

Why a Baby's sense of smell is so important, Pathways.org, www. pathways.org/babys-sense-of-smell/.

PHYSICAL DEVELOPMENT

Dr Christopher Green, 1988, *Babies – A Parents' Guide to Surviving (and Enjoying!) Baby's First Year*, pages 181 – 182, Simon & Schuster Australia.

Fine Motor Development Chart, Kid Sense, https://childdevelopment. com.au/resources/child-development-charts/fine-motor-developmental-chart/.

Gross Motor Development Chart, Kid Sense, https://childdevelopment. com.au/resources/child-development-charts/gross-motor-developmental-chart/.

SPEECH AND LANGUAGE

Dr. Charles E. Schaefer and Theresa Foy DiGeronimo 2000, Ages and Stages, pages 26–8, Published by John Wiley & Sons, Inc.

Speech Sounds Development Chart, Kid Sense, https://childdevelopment.com. au/resources/child-development-charts/speech-sounds-developmental-chart/.

INTELLECTUAL DEVELOPMENT

The 4 Stages of Cognitive Development, VeryWellMind, https://www.verywellmind.com/piagets-stages-of-cognitive-development-2795457.

Sensorimotor Stage of Cognitive Development, Simply Psychology, https://www.simplypsychology.org/sensorimotor.html.

EMOTIONAL DEVELOPMENT

Sally Goddard Blythe, 2008, *What Babies and Children Really Need*, pages 217–220, Hawthorn Press.

Neurodevelopmental delay (NDD)

Smart Learning Solutions, The INPP Programme (Neuro-Motor Immaturity), https://www.smartlearning.co.nz/inpp-neuro-developmental.

Introduction to INPP, The Institute for Neuro-Physiological Psychology, https://www.inpp.org.uk/.

Welcome to INPP Australia, INPP, https://inppaustralia.com.au/

3

Understanding Primitive Reflexes

Primitive reflexes are automatic involuntary motor responses to specific stimuli exhibited by the normally developing baby but absent in neurologically intact and fully developed adults. They are controlled at the brain stem (where the spinal cord enters the brain) and which is responsible for all of our automatic functions such as heart rate, respiration and temperature control. They are inhibited by the developing brain between six to twelve months after birth.

After conception, the tiny cell is already developing its own potential. Within the uterus, the foetus develops primitive reflexes to:

1. enhance its chance of survival;
2. protect foetal development; and
3. assist the baby with the bombardment of new sensory information during the birthing process.

Within the first year these primitive reflexes are gradually taken over by actions known as postural reflexes or postural control. Developmental milestones such as crawling, sitting, standing, walking, etc. play a big role in developing the brain's interconnections — for example, motor development is reliant on neuro development. As the baby adapts to its new environment postural reflexes integrate into the advancing brain. However, if one or more primitive reflexes are retained behavioural problems, learning difficulties and poor posture may arise.

Retained primitive reflexes are inhibited through movement and sensory integration which enables the child to build a stable foundation on which to learn.

Effects in general on retained Primitive Reflexes

- Poor muscle tone, balance, fine motor skills, gross motor skills and posture.
- Midlines are often not integrated: Crossing the midline is when we use the left and right sides of our body together. Integration of midlines is important to effortlessly perform motor tasks such as putting shoes and socks on, kicking and throwing a ball, cutting with scissors, writing and reading.
- Child may be mixed dominant: Mixed dominance is when a child doesn't show a strong preference to either the right or left side of their body with their hand, foot, eye and ear. For example, a child may have a strong preference to using their right hand for drawing and kick a ball with their left foot.
- Child will often find ways to compensate for difficulties they are experiencing.
- Child may be easily startled.
- Child may be overly sensitive to either noise, touch or lighting.
- Child may have low self-esteem.

Moro Reflex

The moro reflex emerges approximately nine weeks in-utero, is fully present at birth and is inhibited between two and four months of age. It is the baby's startle reflex that triggers the 'fight and flight' response. The 'fight and flight' response activates the sympathetic nervous system, causing instantaneous arousal and rapid inhalation, freeze/startled, followed by crying.

If retained too long the moro reflex may cause:

- rapid breathing, increased heart rate and increased blood pressure;
- reddening of skin;
- the child to be easily triggered, with possible emotional outburst, anger or tears;
- poor visual perception;
- auditory confusion;
- vision, reading and writing difficulties;
- difficulty adapting to change;
- low self-esteem;
- poor decision making, stamina, attention and concentration;
- tense muscle tone; and
- sensitivity to bright light.

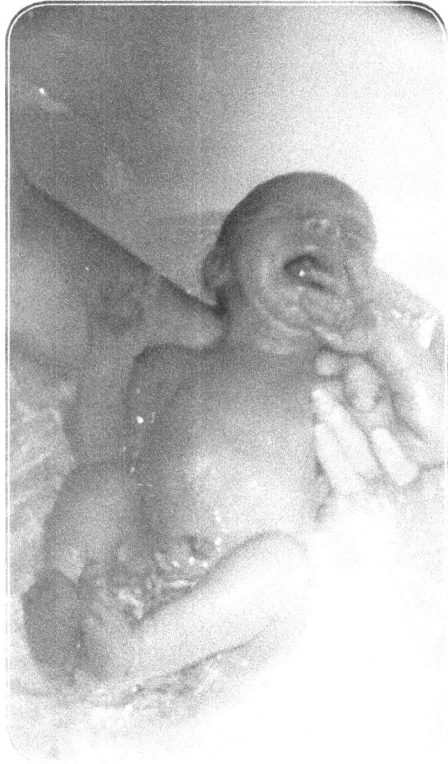

Tonic Labyrinthine Reflex (TLR)

The TLR develops in-utero, is present at birth and is inhibited gradually from six months to three years of age. It acts as the flexor and extensor muscle and responds to movement of the head forwards and backwards.

If retained the TLR can present the following difficulties:

- vestibular difficulties, in particular poor balance and motion sickness;
- a child may tire easily and will need to make a more conscious effort to maintain posture, balance and a stable visual field;
- poor muscle tone;
- poor posture – stooped, walking on tip toes, sliding down on their seat;
- vision, speech and auditory difficulties;
- poor time perception, management and organisation;
- spatial awareness difficulties, sequencing and remembering things;
- visual and perceptual difficulties;
- a dislike of sporting activities; and
- dysfunctional eye movements, and difficulty reading and copying from an electronic whiteboard in the classroom.

Palmar Reflex

The palmar reflex emerges approximately 11 weeks in-utero, is fully present at birth and is inhibited at around three months of age.

This reflex needs to be inhibited for the development of voluntary reaching, the pincer grasp and mobility of the fingers.

If retained the following symptoms may be displayed:

- immature palmar grip;
- poor fine motor skills and mobility of fingers;
- poor manual dexterity and pencil grip; and
- movements with the mouth when writing or drawing — Babkin response. This may cause speech difficulties which shows the continued link between the hand and the mouth.

ASYMMETRICAL TONIC NECK REFLEX (ATNR)

The ATNR plays an active role from 18 weeks in-utero until approximately six months of age. It stimulates the vestibular, helps develop muscle tone and balance and facilitates movement. If the ATNR is retained beyond six months, the following symptoms can result:

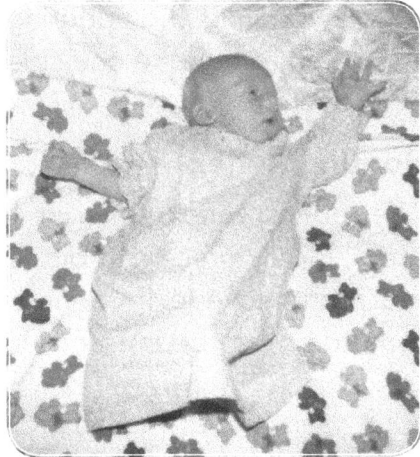

- poor eye tracking;
- difficulty copying from a whiteboard;
- dyslexia;
- reading, listening, handwriting, written expression and spelling;
- difficulty with maths;
- may use fingers when eating;
- poor hand-eye coordination;
- poor balance and an imbalance of tension in muscles when the head is turning; and
- difficulty crossing the midline — the child may not display a cross pattern movement when walking, marching or skipping.

Spinal Galant

The spinal galant reflex emerges approximately 20 weeks in-utero, is actively present at birth and inhibited between three and nine months of age. It assists with the birthing process and may help with sound conduction through the spinal column. If retained beyond nine months the spinal galant reflex may be seen in the following symptoms:

- poor attention, concentration and short-term memory;
- poor bladder control and bedwetting;
- wriggling and fidgeting; and
- hip rotation to one side when walking.

Rooting Reflex

The rooting reflex emerges between 24 and 28 weeks in-utero, is fully present at birth and inhibited at approximately four months of age. If retained after four months, the following symptoms may be present:

- sensitivity to touch around the mouth area;
- difficulties with chewing and swallowing — tongue may be too far forward in the mouth and have immature movements;
- increased arching of palate (cathedral palate), which may result in orthodontic treatment needed at a later stage;
- dribbling;
- poor manual dexterity (Babkin response); and
- speech and articulation difficulties.

Symmetrical Tonic Neck Reflex (STNR)

The STNR is a bridging reflex and appears at around six to nine months of age. This reflex helps develop strength and coordination, as well as training the eyes to work together.

The following symptoms may be present if this reflex isn't integrated:

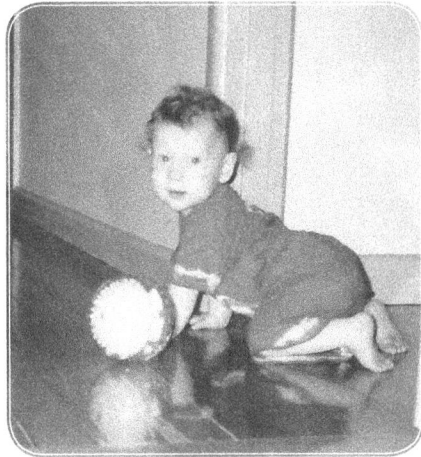

- low muscle tone and stooped posture;
- difficulty with writing and reading;
- slouching when sitting on a chair and a poor attention span;
- difficulty with fine motor control of the wrist and fingers and a messy eater;
- clumsy at ball games and sport with poor swimming skills; and
- slowness at copying tasks.

Chapter Resources

Sally Goddard, 2005, Reflexes, Learning and Behaviour, A Window into the Child's Mind, Fern Ridge Press.

Introduction to INPP, The Institute for Neuro-Physiological Psychology, www.inpp.org.uk.

Enabling every child to learn, Move to Learn, www.movetolearn.com.au.

Ian McGowan, https://uk.linkedin.com/in/ian-mcgowan-b1556721, ian@mlcscotland.com.

FRAME
1 – 3.5 YEARS OLD

Postural reflexes, senses & balance.

FRAME
3.5 – 5 YEARS OLD

Further physical development & integration.

4

Understanding Postural Reflexes

Postural reflexes are a mature response, developed through movement to support the control of balance, posture and movement in a gravity-based environment. They are divided into two groups — known as righting reflexes and equilibrium reactions — and once primitive reflexes are put to sleep, postural reflexes operate on a subconscious level.

If the postural reflexes are underdeveloped, an individual will show signs of difficulty with their balance and motor coordination.

Righting Reflexes

These reflexes start to appear after a child is born and should remain throughout life. As the child grows and their body matures the righting reflexes are important for helping the body adapt when it encounters a sudden loss of balance. It is particularly beneficial for assisting the child's progression through developmental milestones and learning to control their head.

Neck Righting Reflex

This reflex is present in a full-term baby and is one of the first righting reflexes to emerge. Within its first few months, a baby typically makes lots of stretching movements using the muscles in the neck to activate this reflex. When the baby is around three months and developing normally, this reflex can be seen when the baby is lying on their back and they try and do what looks like a log roll — when the baby's head is turned to one side their body will try to move at the same time.

Labyrinthine Head Righting Reflex (LHRR)

This postural reflex is at its height from approximately ten months of age and helps the eyes focus forward in line with the ears. It also plays a role in maintaining the head in an upright position using input from the vestibular system and sensations from the body. This input also helps adjust the posture when the body moves, ensuring that the head remains in the midline position of the body.

Oculo-Head Righting Reflex (OHRR)

The OHRR reflex helps the head remain in a stationary state when the body is moving. It is controlled in the cortex area of the brain and helps the eyes stay focused and in line with the body.

Segmental Rolling Reflexes

Segmental rolling reflexes are postural reflexes which emerge at approximately seven months of age and are refined and integrated into the body for mature postural responses. They help facilitate the sequence of development of sitting, creeping and standing as well as a fluent rolling movement.

If underdeveloped, they result in difficulties with stiff body movements when changing positions, particularly rolling, running and jumping.

Landau Reflex

The landau reflex emerges at approximately two to four months and is inhibited by three years of age. It is a bridging reflex that helps to increase and strengthen muscle tone when in the prone position.

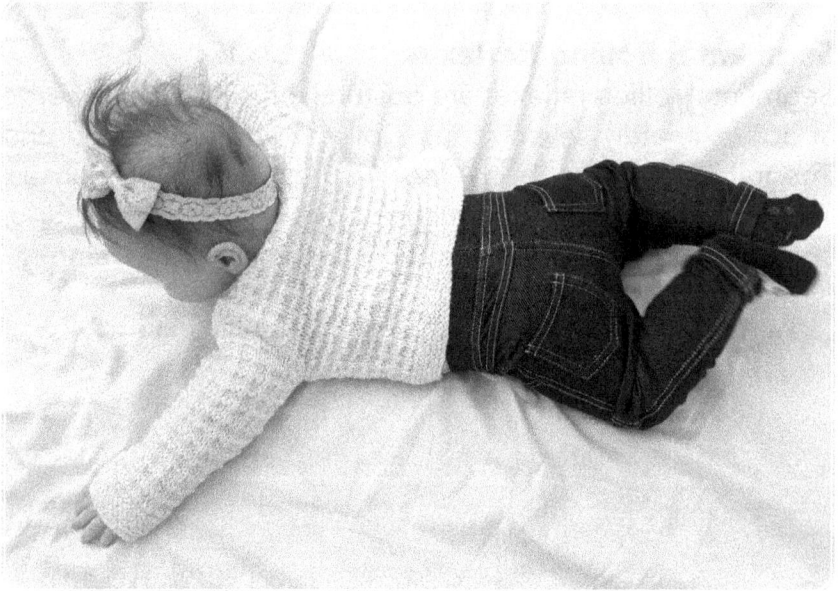

If retained longer than necessary, the following symptoms may appear:

- running stiffly and awkwardly;
- difficulty with skipping, jumping and hopping; and
- poor balance when trying to rapidly change movement during an activity.

Amphibian Reflex

The amphibian reflex emerges between four and six months old and is refined and integrated into a more mature postural response rather than inhibited. It assists with mobility and allows for the independent movement of arms and legs needed for crawling, creeping and gross motor coordination.

If underdeveloped the amphibian reflex may:

- impede the cross-pattern movements in crawling and creeping;
- affect gross motor coordination later in life; and
- cause difficulties with physical education sports.

Equilibrium Reactions

Equilibrium reactions emerge between the age of six and twelve months and are the last of the postural reflexes to present as mature responses. They are needed to maintain balance in the trunk and lower limbs so arms are free for skilled manipulation. At the same time, these reactions are necessary in assisting the body to move freely in different directions, as well as fine tuning precise movements. These precise movements are controlled through both the cortex and cerebellum.

Underdeveloped equilibrium reactions may cause:

- poor balance;
- difficulty with upright posture and slouching when sitting on a chair;
- difficulty with gross motor coordination;
- difficulty with sporting activities, running, jumping, hopping and riding a bike;
- tendency to tire easily as postural adjustments are not automatic; and
- cognitive ability and learning may be affected.

Chapter Resources

Sally Goddard, 2005, *Reflexes Learning and Behaviour, A Window into the Child's Mind*, Fern Ridge Press.

Introduction to INPP, The Institute for Neuro-Physiological Psychology, www.inpp.org.uk.

Postural Reflexes, NeuroRestart – Therapy for immature reflexes, www.neurorestart.co.uk/postural-reflexes/.

Enabling Every Child to Learn, Move to Learn, www.movetolearn.com.au.

Ian McGowan, https://uk.linkedin.com/in/ian-mcgowan-b1556721 and ian@mlcscotland.com.

5

Wired Through Movement

Movement is a child's first language. Before a baby learns to speak single words, they need plenty of time to learn control and movement of their bodies through floor time, and plenty of sensory experiences by observing their world through their senses.

From birth to the age of three and a half years, babies and infants use movement to explore their world, gain control over their body and put primitive reflexes to sleep. This motor development, particularly during the first year of life, should follow a strict chronological sequence which is roughly the same for every child.

Before a child can gain complete control of their whole body, they must first attain head control, so normal development follows a sequence of:

1. From head to chest (torso)
2. From toes to chest (torso)
3. From centre outwards

When building a house, the most important phase in the structure is the foundation level. For childhood development, the foundational level is the primitive reflexes being put to sleep as the baby learns to control their body so that higher centres of the brain can take over. As such, developmental milestones such as rolling, crawling, sitting, standing, and walking, play a major role in developing the brain's interconnections, as, for example, motor development is reliant on neurodevelopment.

Below is a picture taken from The Urban Child Institute, which shows the neural networks from a newborn to an adult. This diagram shows the neural connections are becoming stronger at nine months. By age two, these networks have further developed and become stronger thanks to the baby having floor time and the continual development of their balance system after they learn to walk. Interestingly, the diagram shows that a two-year-old brain has twice as many neural networks as an adult brain.

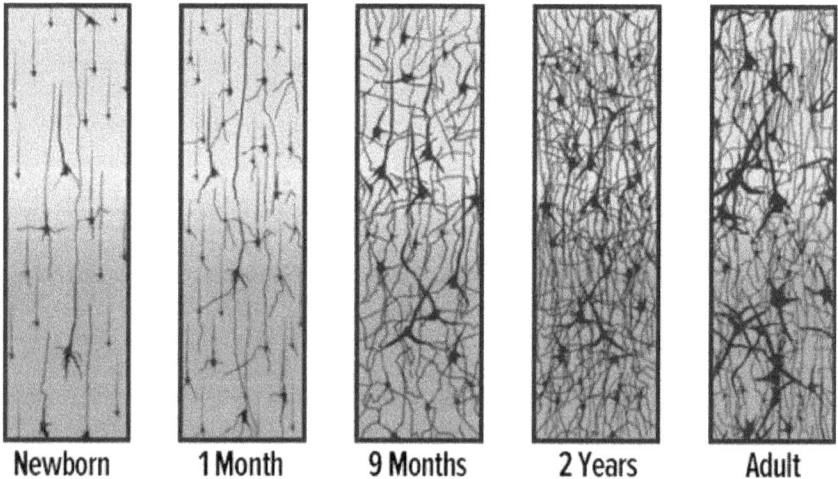

| Newborn | 1 Month | 9 Months | 2 Years | Adult |

Physical Activity for Children – Zero to Two Years

Through my experience and vast knowledge gained through training in various movement programs, I have learnt the importance of physical activity in children aged zero to two years. Lots of free movement and exploration of the world around, both indoors and outdoors, is crucial for babies and toddlers to lay a strong neurological foundation. It is through developmental milestones — such as rolling, reaching, crawling on the stomach, sitting, rocking, creeping, pulling up and walking — that babies and toddlers have an opportunity to use their major muscles and develop muscle tone.

Before walking, babies are programmed to stretch and play. Tummy time provides babies with an opportunity to practice, learn about the world around them and develop strong neck muscles. Australian standards recommend approximately 30 minutes of tummy time over the duration of the day.

During tummy time, physical development can be encouraged by placing a toy or object on the floor so that the baby tries to use more force and effort reaching for it. To assist with strengthening the muscles down and through the neck, try clapping, singing and shaking a toy to encourage the baby to turn its head.

Rolling

Rolling on the floor is beneficial as it stimulates the asymmetrical tonic neck reflex (see Chapter 3 for more information), vestibular and head righting reactions. This allows the baby to move the body to learn that the head must move independently of the body.

Gliding or Parachuting on the Stomach

Gliding or parachuting on the stomach is a stage of development that helps the body work against gravity. It also works on integrating the tonic labyrinthine reflex (see Chapter 3 for more information) in the extension position, as well as helping break up any residual asymmetrical tonic neck reflex.

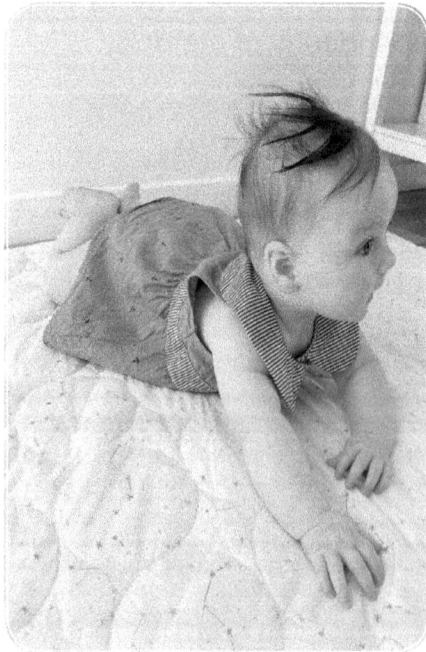

Stomach Crawling

Stomach or commando crawling further strengthens the neck and shoulders in preparation for hand-eye work when taking the next step of integrating the ATNR and TLR reflexes. It also promotes both sides of the body working together through bilateral integration.

Sitting

The baby will learn to sit without support anywhere between four to seven months of age. They will have typically progressed through rolling their bodies over, crawling on their tummy and being able to hold their head up.

Rocking

Rocking on all fours is the step before crawling on hands and knees. Moving back and forth in a rocking motion helps further strengthen the arm and leg muscles, as well as helping integrate the STNR and palmer reflexes. Once the infant gains further strength from this rocking phase they will begin to propel themselves forward using their arms and legs.

Crawling on Hands and Knees

Now an infant's arms and legs have become stronger, the crawling phase encourages the arms and legs on each side to work separately from one another. It also encourages hand-eye coordination, gross and fine motor skills, balance and strength.

Crawling on all fours is an important stage in developing bilateral integration and connecting the senses. It is this stage of development that connects the visual, vestibular and proprioceptive (spatial awareness) systems.

The more the baby crawls on hands and knees, the stronger the networks and connections between the sensory systems become, particularly the sense of balance, spatial awareness and depth perception.

Walking

Once the baby is up and walking, it is extremely beneficial for the child to have lots of opportunities to move and explore the world, for example, time out of the stroller, playing games like hide and seek and looking for objects in the garden.

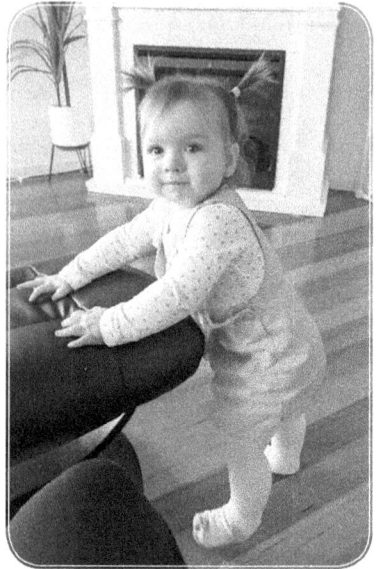

Swinging and spinning on equipment at the park is great for developing both the vestibular system and postural reflexes, and other activities at the park that involve climbing can help build self-confidence and further enhance the balance system in preparation for climbing up and down stairs.

Physical Activity for Children — Two to Five Years

This next phase of development focusses on further strengthening and developing gross motor skills, through time and opportunities to run and play in different surroundings. Great places to do this are the beach, park, bush, playgrounds and swimming.

As well as learning through play at the park and the beach, there are some great physical and social activities parents and children can do together. These not only further enhance the child's physical development but can provide great socialisation with other families in the local community. Two that I recommend from personal experience are water familiarisation (swimming) and Leaping Lizards. Below is a brief overview of these programs.

Water Familiarisation (Swimming)

Baby swim classes are often called water familiarisation and involve the parent and child being in the water together with a qualified instructor. These infant classes help encourage physical development and body awareness, as well as social and emotional interaction.

This fun physical group activity can start from approximately six months old and can promote stronger brain connections as the infant learns to control their bodies in the water. Instructors will encourage parents to assist their child to move freely in the water through fun and interesting games using a variety of interactive and engaging water toys and singing songs.

Many pools offer these classes or something similar, so check with a local pool in your area.

Leaping Lizards

Leaping Lizards has been around for 28 years and is an activity program that aims to enhance a child's natural physical ability. There are three programs catering for sixteen months to three years old, for Kinder groups and for school-aged children. All programs are inclusive for children with extra needs.

These sessions encourage confidence and are designed to stimulate fine and gross motor skills. They are structured and have free play time, as well as allocated practise, and use a circuit of climbing equipment to encourage large muscle movement.

1. The sixteen months to three-year-old program is a 45-minute teacher guided session with both the carer and child participating in fun and stimulating exercises to enhance overall motor development. There is time within this program for exercises to music, as well as for physical activities using small equipment.

2. The Leaping Lizards Kinder program is a one-hour session where the child usually attends without the parent/carer. This class is particularly beneficial as it complements traditional three-and four-year-old Kinder programs by providing further gross motor development, as well as cognitive, social and emotional stimulation.

3. The School Program offers a different sport each term, with approximately ten sports offered over a three-year cycle.

Chapter Resources

BRAIN DIAGRAM

Synapses Density Over Time, The Urban Child Institute, www. urbanchildinstitute.org/why-0-3/baby-and-brain.

PHYSICAL ACTIVITY OF ZERO TO TWO

Physical Activity for Children 0–2 Years, Raising Children — The Australian Parenting Website, https://raisingchildren.net.au/ babies/play-learning/active-play/physical-activity-for-young-children#physical-activity-for-children-0-2-years-nav-title.

SITTING

Developmental Milestones Sitting, Babycenter, www.babycenter.com/ a6505/develomental-milestones-sitting.

ROCKING

Baby Developmental Milestones: By 8 to 12 months, Grow by WebMD, www.webmd.com/parenting/baby/baby-milestones-8-12-months#1.

CRAWLING ON ALL FOURS

Sally Goddard, 2005, *Reflexes, Learning and Behaviour – A Window into the Child's Mind*, page 23, Fern Ridge Press,

PHYSICAL ACTIVITY 2 TO 5 YEARS

Suitable for 0-5 years, Physical activity for young children, Raising Children —The Australian Parenting Website, https://raisingchildren.net.au/ babies/play-learning/active-play/physical-activity-for-young-children.

LEAPING LIZARD

Welcome to Leaping Lizards, Leaping Lizards, www.leapinglizards.com.au.

WATER FAMILIARISATION

Water Familiarisation, Bulleen Swim Centre & Genazzano Swim School, http://www.swimcentre.com/page_water-familiarisation.html

6

Discover the Senses

Humans live in a three-dimensional world, and our five main senses are the pathways to the brain. They help us learn, understand and perceive the physical world around us, and are commonly known as hearing, sight, smell, taste and touch.

There are two other non-traditional senses that play an important role in our environment.

They are the vestibular, which relates to our movement and balance, and proprioception, which refers to the position of our body.

It is important to look at our two non-traditional senses, as they both have a strong relationship and link with our five main senses.

The Five Main Senses

The senses travel to the brain in a way that is similar to how a computer works. Our senses are the input source, and after the brain has processed this sensory information it is presented as a sensory motor output.

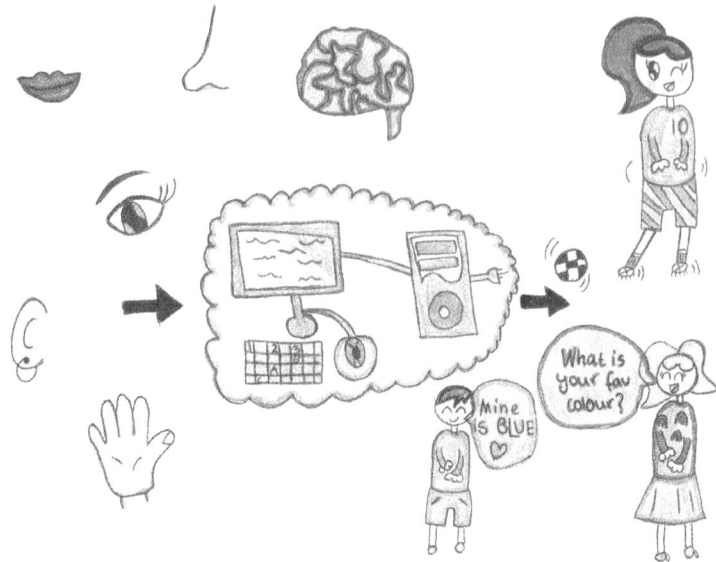

They play a critical role in perception and behaviour, allowing us to make sense of our environment, as well as helping us react to a situation and respond appropriately.

Sensory Inputs	Sensory Outputs
• Auditory	• Speaking
• Visual	• Expressing thoughts
• Tactile	• Moving fluently
• Taste	• Reading
• Smell	• Social behaviour

Auditory (Hearing)

The auditory system is a person's sense of hearing. The ear acts as a receiver, collecting acoustic information and passing it through the nervous system into the brain accurately and efficiently. The ear also includes structures for the sense of balance.

Our auditory system allows us to listen and follow instructions in different environments by perceiving sounds at different frequencies around us. An optimal sense of hearing allows us to perceive different vibrations, tones and sounds and locate where they are coming from — for example, leaves rustling, birds tweeting, and noises in the street.

Auditory perception comes from being able to recognise, understand and assign meaning to a particular sound. If there are difficulties in perceiving sounds accurately potential auditory challenges may be evident. Some common indicators of auditory processing challenges can be noted as a person being either hypersensitive or hyposensitive.

Below is a table showing common indicators of auditory difficulties in both categories.

Hypersensitive	Hyposensitive
• Distracted by sounds • Fearful of sounds • Very sensitive to loud or very sudden noises — may cover ears • Sensitive to a teacher's voice • Doesn't like background noise • Irritated by low intense sounds like fans, heaters or clocks ticking	• Difficulty locating where sound is coming from • May not hear certain sounds • May talk to self throughout a task, often out loud • Difficulty differentiating between words e.g. log and lock • Repeatedly says 'what' • Turns the volume up on the TV or radio

Visual (Sight)

The visual system is the part of the nervous system which allows us to see. Information is interpreted from visible light, allowing an individual to understand and perceive the world around them.

The occipital lobe receives impulses from the optic nerve when light passes through the eyes — basically the eyes look, and the brain sees.

An important note is that the eyes and ears are connected. This connection plays an important role when reading, writing and in our visual perception.

Visual perception can be separated into five categories known as: position in space; visual-motor coordination; form consistency; figure-ground perception; and perception of spatial relations.

A good sense of sight allows us to identify differences in light and movement, and different shapes and colours in our world.

Therefore, good balance and clear vision needs strong neurological connections between the vestibular organs and the eyes. Below is a diagram showing some common indicators of visual difficulties.

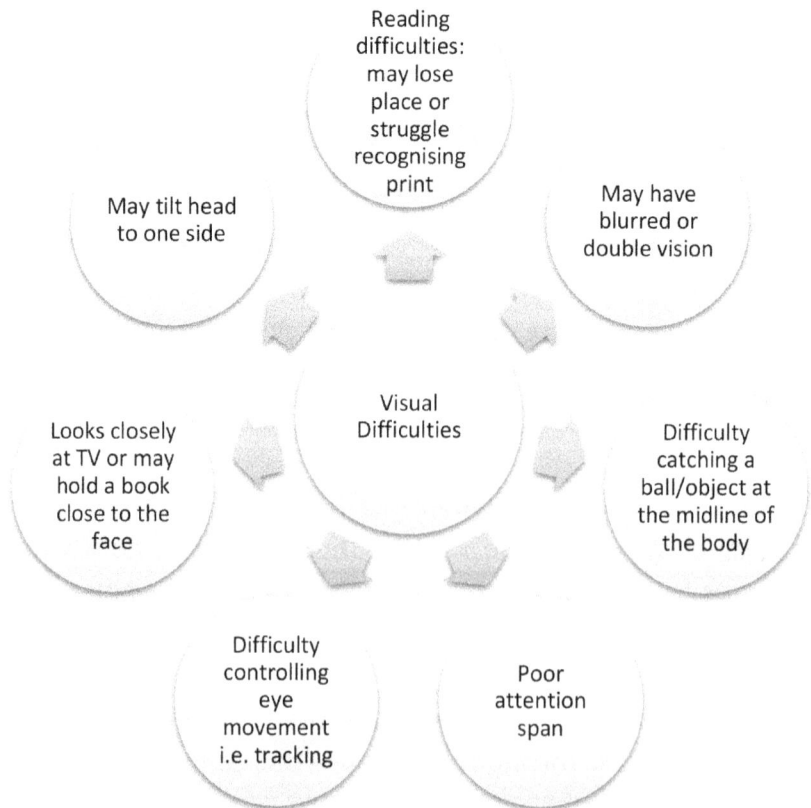

Reading difficulties: may lose place or struggle recognising print

May have blurred or double vision

May tilt head to one side

Looks closely at TV or may hold a book close to the face

Visual Difficulties

Difficulty catching a ball/object at the midline of the body

Difficulty controlling eye movement i.e. tracking

Poor attention span

Tactile (Touch)

The tactile sense is received through millions of nerve endings on the skin. These nerve endings send information — which includes pain, temperature, pressure and texture — to the brain. Within the brain, the parietal lobe receives information when the sense of touch is activated.

Once this happens, neurons along the spinal cord convey the many impulses it receives. The sense of touch provides individuals with information needed for visual perception, motor planning, body awareness, academic learning and social and emotional wellbeing. Below is a diagram showing common symptoms of tactile defensiveness and some suggested activities to stimulate this sense can be found in Chapter 10.

May avoid contact sports such as soccer, football or basketball

May display aggressive behaviour or be labelled a trouble maker

May feel anxious if their feet are off the ground

Tactile Defensiveness

Dislikes having dirty hands

Doesn't like being touched — slightest touch may be painful

Doesn't like firm, fitted clothing

May dislike being dried by a bath or beach towel

Oral (Taste)

Taste is also referred to as gustation and helps us perceive and recognise different flavours from food or drink.

Our taste is detected through taste buds on our tongue and within our mouth and throat, which send messages to our frontal lobe which gives us our sense of taste — flavours are also recognised through our sense of smell. The four basic taste sensations are sweet, sour, bitter and salty.

Below is a table showing common symptoms of taste or oral dysfunction which can be either present as hypersensitivity or hyposensitivity.

Hypersensitive	Hyposensitive
• May gag on certain textured foods • Prefer to eat foods that are blended or soft in texture • Difficulty with sucking, swallowing and/or chewing • Fearful of going to the dentist and doesn't like teeth being brushed • May prefer to eat simple/bland foods • May be a picky eater • May refuse to eat certain foods: salty, sweet or spicy	• May prefer foods with an intense flavour • Constantly chews/sucks on fingers, hair or clothing • Hard to distinguish between different tasting foods • Excessive drooling beyond the teething stage of development • May seek out licking, tasting, sucking and or chewing inedible objects

The Extra Senses

It is also important to look at our two non-traditional senses, the vestibular and proprioception, as these both have a strong relationship and link with our five main senses.

The Vestibular System

The vestibular system develops in-utero, providing almost all the sensory input a developing foetus's brain receives, and appears to be well developed by approximately the fifth month.

The baby stimulates their vestibular system in the womb — which is classified as a non-gravity environment — via movement, and the system is well developed at birth. Inside the womb the baby has been developing and moving in a cosy, warm, safe and secure environment. At birth, the baby is born into a gravity environment, surrounded by lots of sensory information.

For the vestibular system to develop/mature in a gravity world it needs to be activated/stimulated through dynamic movement.

The vestibular is described as our body's internal guidance system and helps us know where our bodies are in relation to the world around us. It orientates both our auditory and visual systems and helps us stand upright, maintain balance and move through space.

The vestibular system is a bony labyrinthine in the inner ear comprising of semicircular canals and otolith organs. It functions automatically at the brain stem level and is stimulated in three different planes of movement: horizontal, vertical, and diagonal.

It also helps us understand the difference between up, down, right and left, as well as the shapes of letters 'b' and 'p', and 'd' and 'q'.

Within the developing brain the vestibular system sends information to our central nervous system for processing, in order to produce muscle tone, and move our bodies in a fluent and organised way.

It also supports our head in space which assists with the proper functioning of the eyes, helping them align and focus together, as well as assisting the ears to localise sound and process what we are hearing.

There are many issues that can affect an individual's learning, concentration, behaviour, and sports performance as a result of a dysfunctional vestibular system. Vestibular dysfunction can present as the following difficulties:

- vestibular sensation perceived in the inner ear is not processed effectively;
- poor ability to integrate information about movement, gravity, balance and where they are in space;
- poor balance when tested with either eyes open or closed;
- oversensitivity or under sensitivity to movement;
- awkward and uncoordinated gross and fine motor movements;
- difficulty with eye-hand coordination at times;
- poor posture, spatial awareness and body geography;
- difficulties with visual, auditory and language tasks; and
- difficulties with behaviour, attention and socialising.

A dysfunctional vestibular can either be under sensitive (hypo vestibular) or oversensitive (hyper vestibular) with their response.

Below is a table showing some common symptoms. Suggested activities to help the vestibular system can be found in Chapter 10 page 114.

Hypersensitive	Hyposensitive
• Doesn't like watching or doing spinning activities • May feel anxious if their feet are off the ground • Tends to move quite slowly and prone to motion sickness • Avoids playgrounds and doesn't like being upside down • Poor motor coordination and may show rigid body movements • Prefer to do activities sitting still like reading • Avoids sports activities and physical education at school	• Poor postural control and body awareness • Usually a daredevil that can't sit still • Fidgets, appears clumsy and accident prone • Seeks out intense, fast and rocking movement activities • Enjoys hanging upside down • May crash or bump into people or things

The Proprioceptive System

Proprioception is the sense of knowing where your body is in space and how much effort and force is required to move the limbs.

It is also referred to as the sixth sense and plays an important role in how our body plans a movement and where our joints are positioned. It mainly occurs at a subconscious level and requires very little thinking.

Proprioception relies on the five main senses as well as the vestibular system to help the brain process necessary information. Proprioception is stimulated by muscle activation through push and pull activities, jumping and stomach crawling. Jumping and stomach crawling can be good for a child who might be disorganised or feeling stressed as it may help to calm the central nervous system down.

It provides information about how much force is required to perform an activity/exercise while maintaining a good state of balance. It also sends messages to the brain relating to the positioning of different body parts, how joints move, the pressure felt on the skin, pain felt in joints, as well as temperature.

Here are examples of different activities requiring varying amounts of force and control.

- Holding a cup
- Serving a tennis ball
- Holding a pencil/pen and writing
- Sitting still in a chair
- Clapping hands
- Throwing a cricket ball
- Swimming different strokes in the water
- Balancing on one leg
- How high to jump to rebound a basketball
- Pulling weeds out of the garden
- Knitting with needles
- Balancing on ice skates
- Playing a musical instrument

Proprioception works very closely with the Vestibular and Visual systems in order to assist with helping us to keep our bodies in a balanced state and upright position. If for example one of these three systems is underdeveloped or not functioning at a normal level, then two systems will automatically take over.

For example, a child who is blind will totally rely on their proprioceptive and vestibular systems to help their body maintain balance.

On the other hand, if an individual has an under-developed vestibular system they will most likely have poor proprioception and as a result their visual system will dominate to let the body know where it is in space.

When the visual system is solely relied upon to remain in the upright position, then it can quite often be seen that the individual becomes tired, distracted and possibly irritable.

Below is a diagram showing some common symptoms.

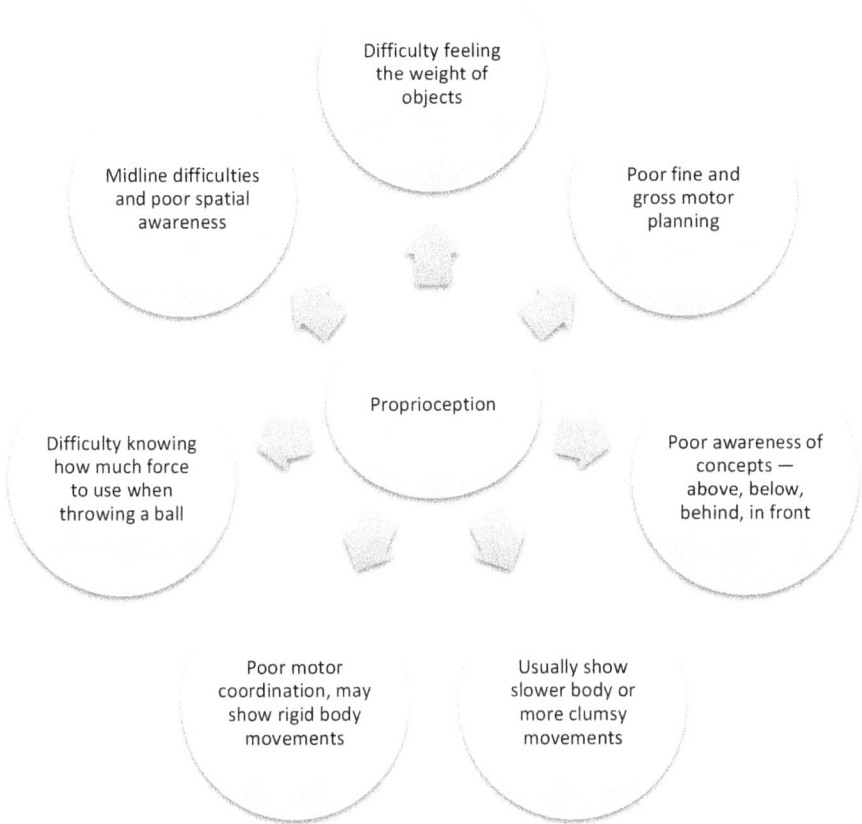

Difficulty feeling the weight of objects

Midline difficulties and poor spatial awareness

Poor fine and gross motor planning

Difficulty knowing how much force to use when throwing a ball

Proprioception

Poor awareness of concepts — above, below, behind, in front

Poor motor coordination, may show rigid body movements

Usually show slower body or more clumsy movements

Activities to stimulate this sense can be found in Chapter 10.

Chapter Resources

AUDITORY

Willi Aeppli, 2006, *The Care and Development of the Human Senses — Rudolf Steiner's Work on the Significance of the Senses in Education*, page 19, Steiner Schools Fellowship Publications.

Billy Ann Cheatum and Allison A. Hammond, 2000, *Physical Activities for Improving Children's Learning & Behaviour*, page 320, Human Kinetics.

What are the 7 Senses, 7 Senses Foundation, www.7senses.org.au/what-are-the-7-senses/.

VISUAL

Willi Aeppli, 2006, *The Care and Development of the Human Senses — Rudolf Steiner's Work on the Significance of the Senses in Education*, page 15, Steiner Schools Fellowship Publications.

What are the 7 Senses, 7 Senses Foundation, www.7senses.org.au/what-are-the-7-senses/.

TACTILE

What are the 7 senses, 7 Senses Foundation, www.7senses.org.au/what-are-the-7-senses/.

Billy Ann Cheatum and Allison A. Hammond, 2000, *Physical Activities for Improving Children's Learning & Behaviour*, page 242, Human Kinetics.

Tactile Sensitivity, Kid Companions, kidcompanions.com/tactile-sensitivity-what-it-is-and-the-common-signs/.

TASTE

What are the 7 senses, 7 Senses Foundation, www.7senses.org.au/what-are-the-7-senses/

Vestibular.

Billy Ann Cheatum and Allison A. Hammond, 2000, *Physical Activities for Improving Children's Learning & Behaviour*, page 166, Human Kinetics.

The Vestibular System, SPD Australia, https://spdaustralia.com.au/the-vestibular-system/.

PROPRIOCEPTION

7 Senses Street Day, 7 Sense, 7senses.org.au/wp-content/uploads/2013/09/7-Senses-Street-Day-What-are-the-7-Senses_.pdf.

Billy Ann Cheatum and Allison A. Hammond, 2000, *Physical Activities for Improving Children's Learning & Behaviour,* pages 187–188, 205, Human Kinetics.

DIAGRAMS

Created in powerpoint by Jenny Cluning.

DRAWING

Hand drawn by Vanessa Nicoletti.

ROOF
5 – 7 YEARS OLD

Thinking, playing, socialising, learning at school.

7

The Plastic Brain

Neuroplasticity is also known as brain plasticity and is the brain's natural ability to reorganise itself by forming new neural pathways and connections throughout life. As such, the brain can adapt to situations and make changes through different experiences in an individual's environment.

An example of neuroplasticity can be seen if one hemisphere of the brain suffers damage and as a result the other side of the brain will adjust and form connections when a new activity is performed.

Our brain is like a muscle and is shaped through our experiences and forming new neural pathways through repeated actions or experiences. It can be very similar to working with weights at the gym. Building muscle size and strength at the gym usually occurs through repeating a specific set of exercises several times a week. When rewiring the brain, this happens when a goal specific movement action is repeated frequently and intensely in a coordinated fashion. An individual can do certain exercises/activities which stimulate neurons and creates new communications and connections between intact neurons.

The brain has an amazing capacity to expand its neurons and create new pathways. It is very adaptable in many different environments or situations, for example learning at school or playing sport.

This change happens as a result of learning a new skill and improving on it in different environments. Initially, the brain creates a stronger network of neurons, followed by the activation of new neural pathways when learning a new task. This new information needs to be frequently practised regularly over a period of time.

The more I learn and read about neuroplasticity, the more I believe it can benefit all of us. Many decades of research in neuroscience has produced evidence which indicates that the brain has the ability to change through new experiences in both physical structure (anatomy) and function organisation (physiology).

Through writing this book I came across interesting research which supports this. Of particular interest is some fascinating research on the deterioration and recovery of brain damage, which I read through a summary by Associate Professor Jeffrey A. Kleim and Professor Theresa A. Jones. In this, Kleim and Jones came up with ten rules relating to neuroplasticity. Below are dot points of these rules taken from the website, which can be found in the chapter resources, that give a simple explanation of how pliable the brain can be:

- Use it or lose it — failure to drive specific brain functions can lead to functional degradation
- Use it and improve it — training drives brain functions and can lead to enhancement of function
- Specificity — nature of the training experience dictates the nature of the plasticity
- Repetition matters — plasticity requires sufficient repetition
- Intensity matters — plasticity requires sufficient training intensity

- Time matters — different forms of plasticity occur at different times during training and over the course of recovery
- Salience matters —training experience must be sufficiently salient to induce plasticity
- Age matters — plasticity occurs more readily in younger brains; adult brains are capable of plastic adaptation and some degree of structural organization
- Transference — plasticity in response to one training experience can enhance acquisition of similar behaviours
- Interference — plasticity in response to one experience can interfere with the acquisition of other behaviours

A couple of examples of neuroplasticity at work relating to specificity, repetition and intensity are my own experience in my final year at school and a boy aged 13, who was being home schooled for two terms in year seven and received daily one-on-one tutoring for an hour at a time.

When I was in high school, I was interested in sport, music, science and art, and during those years I found reading and writing the most challenging. When writing English essays, I fluctuated between failing the subject and just passing while having weekly support from a tutor. In my final year at school I was managing with all my subjects, except for English. I was determined to pass English so over the last three months leading up to the exams I had tutoring once a week and practised my essay writing twice a day for an hour at a time. This specific task repeated daily in short periods over twelve weeks made me feel confident going into the English exam. Though struggling to pass my essay writing between years ten and twelve, I achieved 75 per cent on my final exam. I truly believe this was a result of practising my essay writing technique through **repetition** and **intensity**.

The second example of neuroplasticity at work is of a 13-year-old boy in year seven who felt very overwhelmed with the jump from grade six to high school.

He was having one-on-one tutoring in both English and Maths once a week which was helping, but his parents decided home schooling for a short period might help their son regain his confidence levels.

A tutor worked with their son daily for an hour at a time and also developed a timetable for him to work on his other subjects. With this routine, over two terms the boy grew in confidence and his stress levels reduced dramatically and he transitioned back to school with confidence and self-belief. In Stories and Testimonials there is a testimonial from this boy's parents on his achievements.

Over the years I have read various books on movement, exercise and neuroplasticity and three of my favourites that I felt were worth sharing in this chapter are: *The Brain that Changes Itself, Spark* and *The Woman Who Changed Her Brain.*

The Brain that Changes Itself by psychiatrist and researcher Dr. Norman Doidge.

This book is touching in so many ways. How Dr. Norman Doidge portrays the personal stories included helps the reader gain a new insight into human potential. In this book there are many case studies of neuroplasticity and several personal stories of triumph. One that stands out for me was that of Dr. Michael Bernstein, an eye surgeon who suffered a stroke and made a remarkable recovery through intensive therapy. The

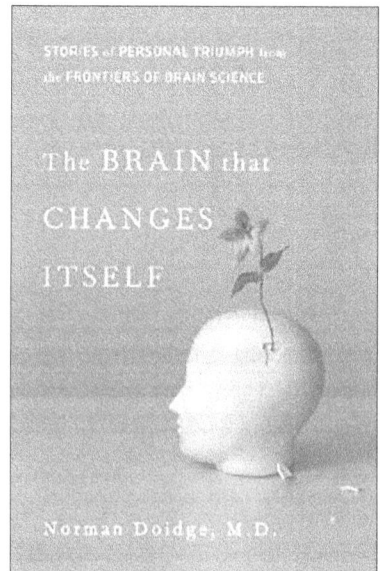

other is of a woman named Michelle Mack who was born with half a brain. In Chapter 11 of his book, Dr. Doidge talks about how Mack was able to rewire her brain to work as a whole through neuroplasticity.

The Brain that Changes Itself is also available on DVD and is basically a documentary that looks at amazing changes that have occurred through the power of neuroplasticity.

There are individuals with learning disorders, as well as those with brain trauma and stroke victims who have shown improvement in their everyday life.

The book *Spark* by John J. Ratey, MD, is a must read for anyone wanting to learn about how the brain can be shaped through exercise and movement. There are lots of case studies and research included to support this.

Ratey reflects on how aerobic exercise activities may help remodel the brain for ultimate performance.

He also details how exercise may help with learning, and individuals with ADHD, mood disorders, Alzheimer's and more.

SPARK

THE REVOLUTIONARY NEW SCIENCE OF EXERCISE AND THE BRAIN

Supercharge Your Mental Circuits to Beat Stress, Sharpen Your Thinking, Lift Your Mood, Boost Your Memory, and Much More

JOHN J. RATEY, MD

COAUTHOR OF *DRIVEN TO DISTRACTION*

with ERIC HAGERMAN

In Chapter 2 under 'Learning', Ratey discusses about a small Japanese scientific study which specifically explored how jogging could improve executive function. This improvement was noticed when jogging for 30 minutes, two to three times a week over a 12-week period.

What I found particularly interesting in this section is that Ratey also stated it was important to include exercises and movements that involved coordination while jogging.

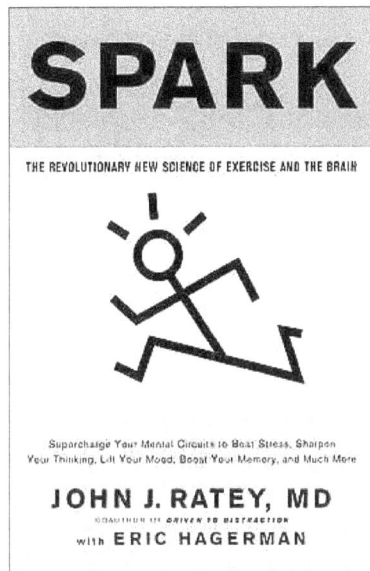

Another great book worth reading is *The Woman Who Changed Her Brain* by Barbara Arrowsmith-Young.

The foreword is written by Dr. Norman Doidge and in the book, Arrowsmith-Young outlines her personal learning struggles she experienced with reading and writing things from right to left, as opposed to left to right.

She used her strong memory skills to complete graduate school and it was only by chance she came across some research. The research she stumbled upon motivated her to develop cognitive exercises to 'fix' her brain and in 1980 she founded the Arrowsmith School in Toronto. After this she developed a program to train teachers from schools across North America in the Arrowsmith methodology.

These resources have helped me to gain a further insight into neuroplasticity and how the brain can build new pathways and stronger connections through specific goal orientated tasks.

From my personal experience using developmental movement and listening therapies with my own children and individual clients, I have witnessed the brain making changes through the repeated practise and learning of a new skill/s, frequently and intensely over a period of time. These changes in individuals can be read in the section 'Bright Futures, Stories and Testimonials'.

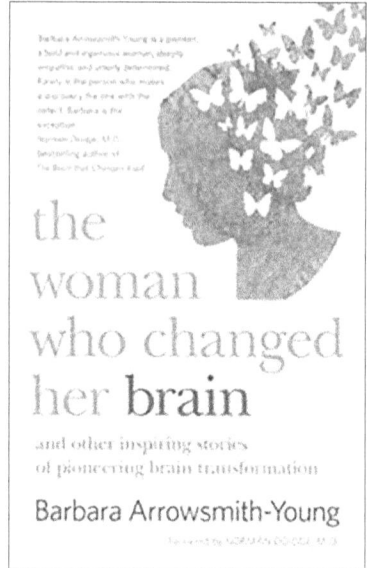

Chapter Resources

Medical Definition of Neuroplasticity, MedicineNet, medicinenet.com/
script/main/art.asp?articlekey=40362.

What is Neuroplasticity?, Brainworks Train Your Mind,
brainworksneurotherapy.com/what-neuroplasticity.

Neuroplasticity, ScienceDirect, www.sciencedirect.com/topics/
neuroscience/neuroplasticity.

Jeffrey A. Kleim, Biological and Health Systems Engineering
Associate Professor, Arizona State University, www.isearch.asu.edu/
profile/1660033.

Theresa A. Jones, Professor, Department of Psychology, The University
of Texas in Austin, www.liberalarts.utexas.edu/psychology/faculty/
jonest10.

BOOK REFERENCES

Norman Doidge M. D., 2007, *The Brain that Changes Itself*, Script
Publications Pty Ltd.

Barbara Arrowsmith-Young, 2012, *The Woman Who Changed Her Brain —
and Other Inspiring Stories of Pioneering Brain Transformation*, Harper
Collins Publishers Australia Pty Limited.

John J. Ratey, MD, 2008, *Spark – The Revolutionary New Science of
Exercise and the Brain*, Little Brown and Company.

8

School Readiness Framework

In this chapter I am going to outline and give an understanding of how a strong physical foundation is important not only for many aspects of our daily life but also for being 'Ready for School'.

What is School Readiness?

School readiness can be defined as a child having a combination of skills, understanding and behaviours that enable them to join in and thrive at school.

When a child goes to school, they need to be independent, have social/emotional maturity, and physical skills as well as language and cognitive skills.

They also need to be able to sit attentively when learning to read, write, spell and perform maths tasks. To be able to learn these 'academic' skills, a child must be developmentally ready as a whole person.

One area that has a crucial role in building a strong foundational base for learning, socialising, following instructions and communicating their needs is a child's physical development.

Being physically ready for school is having:

- integrated primitive reflexes;
- well-developed postural reflexes;
- coordinated gross motor skills – running, jumping, climbing, catching a ball and bilateral integration; and
- mature fine motor skills – holding a pencil or turning pages of a book.

To be a happy learner and play without stress at school or be neuro-motor ready, is to have a strong physical foundation with integrated primitive reflexes, sensory system and a well-developed postural system.

The picture of the Learning House (opposite page), hand-drawn by myself, shows that learning in the classroom uses higher centres of the brain. If there are any gaps neurologically — like partially retained primitive reflexes, poor sensory integration or an underdeveloped postural reflex system — then motor control, learning, behaviour, concentration and P.E. activities become challenging and put stress on an individual's body.

The following is a checklist showing some essential qualities needed to be physically ready for school:

- Smooth and fluent movements when marching, jumping, skipping, hopping, throwing and catching a ball;
- Sitting still on a chair or on the floor without needing to move, fidget or wiggle;
- Balance on one leg for ten seconds with eyes open and eyes closed;
- March or skip cross laterally;
- Draw basic shapes, letters and numbers; and
- Draw a recognisable picture of a person.

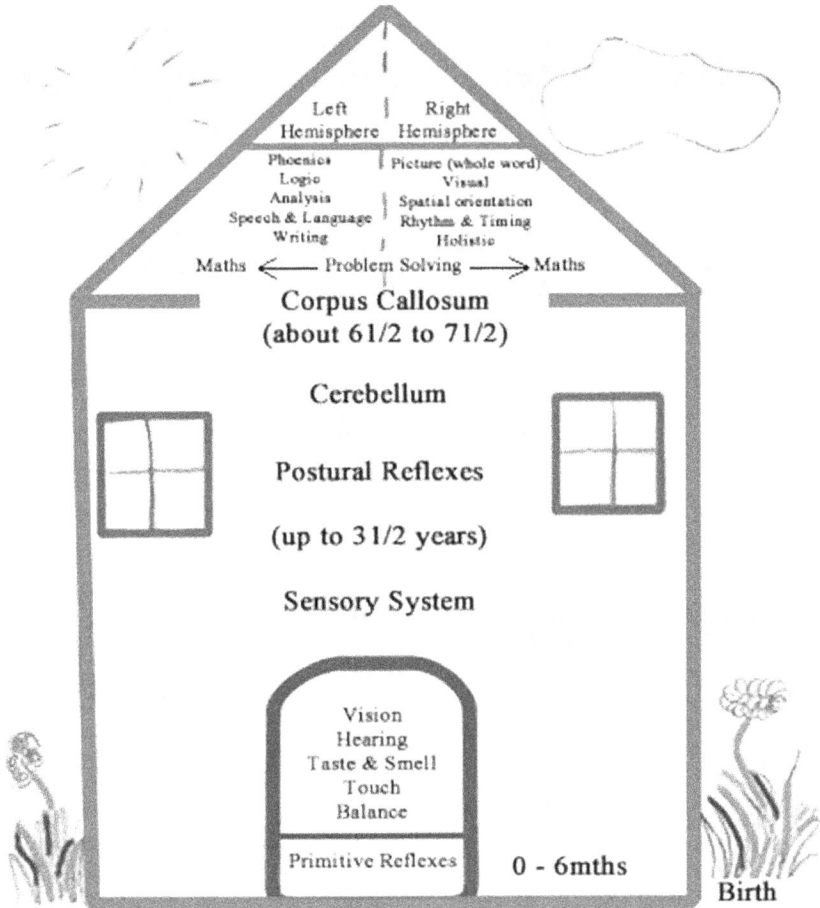

A delay in the sensory motor system, partially retained primitive reflexes or underdeveloped postural reflexes may be present if a child cannot do one or more of the above. Well-integrated vestibular and proprioceptive systems, meanwhile, ensure a child is more attentive and engaged in formal learning and sporting activities.

Learning in a classroom also requires an individual to have good static balance, while sitting still, listening to the teacher and blocking out any visual and auditory distractions around them.

Dynamic and static balance at school and preschool

Dynamic balance is the body's ability to perform efficient and controlled movements when in motion or switching between positions.

Good dynamic balance shows when an individual can competently perform motor tasks like, bike riding, climbing monkey bars, and playing ball sports like basketball, soccer or football.

Static balance, meanwhile, is the ability to remain in one position without having the tendency to rotate because of the force of gravity. Good static balance means a person may be more attentive and engaged in a stationery activity such as sitting in a classroom listening to the teacher.

Children who may withdraw from physical activities requiring movement of the body in space or rapidly changing in direction may have a poorly developed control of dynamic balance.

Individuals with poor static balance instead, may find it difficult to sit still, or be restless and fidgety. For example, a child may have difficulty attending and learning in the classroom because it requires the ability to:

- sit still;
- hold a pencil;
- listen to the teacher;
- process what the teacher has said; and
- block out background noise in the classroom.

The table below shows some fun activities (that are discussed in more detail in Chapter 10) I have found beneficial with learning to read, write and enhance neural pathways.

Activities to assist with learning to read and write	Activities to enhance neural pathways
• Developmental floor movements — (Move to Learn program) • Bean bag and ball exercises • Balancing on one leg • Walking heel to toe along a line or on a balance beam • Naming different body parts • Balloon tapping and clapping rhythms • Animal walks and jumping on a trampoline • Log rolling on the floor • Skipping with a rope	• Picking up marbles with the toes • Animal and peg finger exercises • Cutting with scissors • Drawing and painting • Playing with play dough or shaving foam • Dot to dot activity books • Pulling weeds out in the garden • Finger knitting

The other areas to look at for school readiness, as mentioned earlier, are independence, social skills, emotional maturity, language and cognitive skills.

Independence can be seen when a child is able to manage basic skills such as going to the toilet, being responsible for their own belongings, unwrapping their lunch and dressing confidently.

Social skills can be seen when a child is able to play by themselves as well as with other children of the same age, being able to express their needs, get along with peers and show basic manners.

Emotional Maturity is displayed when a child manages and controls their emotions and understands and copes with new rules placed upon them in their new environment. A child should also be able to focus on a task and follow directions from their teacher.

Language skills is an important area as a child should not only have clear speech but be able to communicate with and listen to other children and their teachers. They should also have the skills to understand stories and begin to identify and recognise the sounds of letters.

Cognitive skills can be seen in a child who is able to play games by taking turns and learning to wait their turn, as well as having a basic understanding of numbers and being able to think through situations.

Being ready for school involves so much more than being independent, cognitively, socially and emotionally prepared. On top of those skills, a strong physical foundation with sensory integration, primitive reflexes that have been put to sleep, and well-developed postural reflexes, is crucial in helping a child to flourish inside and outside of the classroom. A great program that may help children prepare for school by setting this strong foundation is Gymbaroo-Kindyroo.

Gymbaroo-Kindyroo

Gymbaroo-Kindyroo is a parent and child program from birth to five years of age which has been running for nearly 40 years and is available throughout centres in both Australia and overseas. It is research based, using a model that specifically addresses the key developmental stages critical for laying a strong foundation for lifelong learning.

The classes are offered in different age groups, all of which use developmental exercises through music, songs, games and dance.

Gymbaroo-Kindyroo has nine levels of classes, each with a specific program that progresses on developmentally from each other. As well as encouraging physical skills, the age specific classes assist with strengthening social and emotional development, as well as communication and thinking skills.

The classes are guided by a teacher using fun and stimulating activities to support body and brain development and are a great opportunity for local families to socialise and engage with one another.

Chapter resources

BEING READY FOR SCHOOL

Is your child ready for big school?, Learning Potential – Australian Government, www.learningpotential.gov.au/is-your-child-ready-for-big-school.

DYNAMIC AND STATIC BALANCE

Difference Between Static Balance and Dynamic Balancing, Bellwood Rewinds Limited, www.bellwoodrewinds.co.uk/difference-static-balance-dynamic-balancing/.

SCHOOL SKILLS

Is your child ready for big school?, Learning Potential – Australian Government, www.learningpotential.gov.au/articles/is-your-child-ready-for-big-school, Our Programs.

GymbaRoo-KindyRoo, Our Programs, www.gymbaroo.com.au.

DRAWING

Hand drawn by Vanessa Nicoletti.

Neuro Therapy Tool Kit

9

Ultimate Neuro Therapies

In this chapter I outline various developmental movement and listening therapy interventions designed to help children whose early development may have been affected or not unfolded properly. The programs summarised in this chapter may assist with improving:

- focus, concentration and attention;
- literacy and numeracy;
- educational underachievement;
- Attention deficit disorder (ADD)/Attention deficit hyperactivity disorder (ADHD);
- dyslexia or dyspraxia; and
- mild ASD.

To help gain a deeper understanding of each of these programs described below, you can visit their websites (in Chapter Resources) to find out more detailed information on these programs, research, training options and trained practitioners.

Movement Interventions

Developmental movement programs are designed to assist with both integrating any lingering primitive reflexes and further strengthening the sensory systems.

Movements and exercises from the various programs outlined in this chapter can help an individual if they haven't progressed naturally through their milestones or may have not fully integrated their sensory system.

With neuroplasticity, the brain has the capacity to respond quickly to movements that involve bilateral integration, jumping, balancing, motor coordination activities, and fine and gross motor skills. These activities support an individual whose brain/body connections and sensory system may be underdeveloped, by strengthening the neural pathways.

Move to Learn

The Move to Learn program is a simple, flexible movement intervention based on natural movements of babies and toddlers.

Move to Learn was founded in 1987 by Barbara Pheloung, a teacher and specialist in the field of special education. Barbara has spent over 35 years gathering and developing techniques which have helped both her daughter and thousands of other children.

Move to Learn was formed from frustrations Barbara encountered when trying to find help and support for her daughter who struggled with hyperactivity and Learning Difficulties (LD), so she set out to find a solution.

From this, in 1987 Barbara set up The Beach House, a specialised treatment centre in Manly with like-minded teachers and therapists. It was a private centre for individuals with learning difficulties and hyperactivity in which teachers, physiotherapists, occupational therapists and physical education teachers worked together sharing their expertise and helping the community.

Move to Learn comprises ten simple movement activities that cover all essential movement patterns to help establish a strong foundation for effective academic learning, social wellbeing and participating in sport.

The program can be done with an individual, small group or whole class and all that is needed is a copy of '10 Gems for the Brain', or the Move to Learn DVD and some floor space. Illustrative posters are also available.

INPP Method

Dr Peter Blythe (PhD) and Sally Goddard Blythe are experts in the area of NDD (neuro-developmental delay) and have written numerous books on the subject and have pioneered research into NDD. In 1975 they established the Institute for Neuro-Physiological Psychology (INPP).

The INPP programme has been developed as a non-invasive drug free treatment which can help children or adults overcome specific learning challenges.

The treatment comprises a series of physical exercises based on early movements made by developing children in the first year(s) of life. The exercises are designed to retrain the reflex pathways and thereby improve the control of balance, posture, voluntary movement, visual functioning and perceptual abilities.

A typical programme will take about five to ten minutes a day over a period of 12 months. Progress is reviewed at six to eight weekly intervals and exercises are changed when appropriate.

Therapy using INPP is done through practitioners who are trained in the INPP method. Training is also available for health professionals to give them the necessary skills to identify neuro-motor immaturities in individuals.

Bilateral Integration

The original work of Bilateral Integration was developed by Sheila Dobie OBE. Ian McGowan, Director of the Movement and Learning Centre in Scotland, runs training in this method in both Scotland and Melbourne, Australia.

Bilateral Integration is designed to develop coordination and balance, integrate the sensory system and to stimulate the neurological links between movement and cognition.

It can be used as a progressive intervention with individuals with motor or sensory deficits and can also be used in conjunction with '10 Gems for the Brain' from the Move to Learn program.

The Bilateral Integration sequence of movements can also be used in settings such as physical education programs and sports training groups, to facilitate improvement in movement capabilities and enhance not only sports performance, but academic learning.

A typical programme requires approximately five minutes of exercise done daily for a period of 12 months, with exercises changed every four to six weeks.

Extra Lesson®

An Extra Lesson session is a movement therapy program designed to assist children and adolescents with:

- balance and coordination;
- fine and gross motor skills;
- spatial awareness;
- muscle tone;
- reading;
- writing;
- maths;
- memory;
- behaviour;

- concentration;
- self-esteem;
- a short attention span;
- difficulty with relationships;
- emotional regulation; and
- executive functioning and planning.

It is based on the theory that learning difficulties are related to developmental and sensory integration issues from the first seven-year phase of development.

Working from the research of neuroplasticity, the program targets retained primitive reflexes and sequential movement development based on the individual child's development.

It works to establish postural reflexes, dominance/laterality, vestibular functioning, visual-spatial orientation, body geography and spatial orientation, which all help the child improve and reach their potential.

The program involves a trained practitioner working on an individualised intervention program one-on-one with a child on a weekly basis. The length of time varies with each child, but a minimum of 12 months is usually needed to work through any underlying issues.

An Extra Lesson program combines movement, coordination, speech, drawing and painting exercises presented in a way to make the child feel confident, improve their self-esteem, academic performance and social interaction, as well as awakening their imagination and creativity.

The child is also given a set of three to five exercises to practise at home each day — the time spent on this at home should be fun and only takes five to ten minutes.

Rhythmic Movement Training

Rhythmic Movement Training (RMT) is a movement based, primitive (infant or neo-natal) reflex integration programme that uses developmental movements, gentle isometric pressure and self-awareness to rebuild the foundations necessary to overcome learning, sensory, emotional and behavioural challenges.

RMT replicates the developmental movements associated with infant reflexes. It also uses gentle isometric pressure to bring awareness to the body, assisting in releasing stress and learned patterns of behaviour.

RMT looks at the role of developmental movements babies naturally make before birth to six months after birth as they get up on their hands and knees and prepare to learn to walk.

RMT works by integrating the retained or underdeveloped infant reflexes that are involved in learning challenges such as ADD/ADHD, dyslexia, dyspraxia, writing problems, focussing and comprehension challenges, coordination difficulties and Asperger's Syndrome.

BRAIN GYM®

The Brain Gym program was co-developed by Paul E. Dennison Ph.D, and Gail E. Dennison. It has been used for over 40 years in 80 countries by early childhood, primary and secondary educators and comprises 26 basic movements.

These basic activities, used as part of Brain Gym, go back to early movement patterns babies and infants go through when they learn how to coordinate their body, eyes, ears and hands.

The movements are fun and can be used in many different settings by children, adults, special needs groups, school environment, arts and sporting groups, the elderly and with the family at home.

The movements are designed to improve attention, focus, concentration, motor coordination, memory, enhance sports performance, academics — reading, writing, spelling and maths — and organisation.

The Learning Breakthrough Program

The Learning Breakthrough program is a multi-sensory brain training program designed for ages six through to adulthood. Dr. Frank Belgau pioneered this program in 1982 to help integrate motor planning and the sensory system.

It uses specific balance exercises and physical movements in a way which is designed to strengthen basic brain processes while helping organise the way the brain processes sensory information.

The foundation of the program is the unique Belgau Balance Board, which is supported by other equipment to perform a variety of exercises to help improve motor coordination, body awareness, focus, concentration, academic performance and sports performance.

The exercises and physical movements are fun and simple to use, ideally performed over two 15-minute sessions a day. The program schedule is recommended to be on a daily basis over nine to twelve months.

Interactive Metronome

The Interactive Metronome (IM) is an evidence-based training program that measures and improves timing in the brain for cognitive, sensory and motor performance. IM equipment consists of hardware and software, including a master control unit, headphones, hand triggers and foot triggers.

The program challenges an individual to coordinate motor movements in time with a steady metronome beat. Immediate auditory and visual feedback is given — right down to the millisecond — in response to whether the individual is hitting the trigger before, after or at the same time as the reference beat.

The instant feedback provided to the auditory and visual systems allows the individual to make real-time motor movement corrections to perform more accurately. With regular training, an individual can potentially improve their timing and motor rhythm.

On the IM website there are studies and research suggesting improved timing may assist in better overall neurological function, contributing to gains in the following areas:

- concentration and attention;
- executive functioning;
- processing speed;
- self-regulation;
- speech and language — expressive and receptive;
- maths;
- reading — rate, fluency and comprehension;
- upper extremity function (Parkinson's, hemiplegia, cerebral palsy and hand function);
- balance and gait;
- motor coordination; and
- athletic/sports performance.

LISTENING THERAPIES

As well as a varied array of movement therapies there are many listening therapies available. The three I have outlined here are: Johansen Individualised Auditory Stimulation (JIAS), Integrated Listening Systems (iLs) and The Listening Program (TLP).

I have chosen to include these three because I have completed training in them and have had personal experience using them with my own family and clients.

Each of these programs may have great benefits. They may improve concentration, memory, attention, communication skills, written language, motor development, posture, balance, coordination, public speaking skills, and vocabulary.

At the same time, they can reduce anxiety, fatigue, help us control our emotions and provide an individual with more energy.

Johansen Individualised Auditory Stimulation (JIAS)

Johansen Individualised Auditory Stimulation (also known as Johansen Sound Therapy) was developed in Denmark by Dr. Kjeld Johansen, director of the Baltic Dyslexia Research Laboratory, from the original work of Christian A. Volf.

It is a home or school-based sound therapy programme, which involves listening to specially recorded music for ten minutes a day, six days a week, over an average of nine months. JIAS is the only auditory stimulation programme which can customise music to an individual's listening curve to organise and enhance auditory processing skills.

The programme is offered through trained providers. An initial assessment, where an audiogram is taken to show how the left and right ears track against an ideal listening curve, is done, and reviews are a regular part of the program to ascertain necessary changes to a client's listening profile. New music is created following each review according to the updated audiogram.

JIAS may benefit children, adolescents and adults who have difficulty with expressive and receptive language, as well as reading, writing and spelling. Through addressing underlying auditory processing, an individual may notice they are able to discriminate, understand and organise speech sounds better.

Integrated Listening Systems (iLs)

Integrated Listening Systems is a multi-sensory listening therapy program which uses music, movement and language exercises to improve brain function.

This program takes some commitment, assistance and guidance from a parent or carer to complete the program.

It is enjoyable and can be used by itself or together with developmental movement activities/exercises.

The iLs therapy program trains the brain and body through sensory integration followed by more involved cognitive tasks involving speech, language and social skills.

It is offered by trained providers as it requires clinical instruction and supervision. The program length is typically 30 to 60 minutes, two to five times a week and takes anywhere between two and six months to complete.

The Listening Program® (TLP)

The Listening Program® is a neuroscience-based music listening therapy program that stimulates the brain through acoustically modified music, to help performance in school, work and everyday life skills. It can be used with different age groups at different levels ranging from neuro-therapeutic to neuro-wellness and neuro-performance. It is used through trained providers in over 40 countries.

TLP is available on preloaded digital media players and through mobile apps and an online streaming service. It is evidence-based and supported by peer-reviewed research. TLP is used in schools, therapy clinics, hospitals, and the military.

When listening to the scientifically designed music, an individual will preferably use Advanced Brain Technologies' Waves headphones or custom-designed air and bone conduction over-ear headphones.

The structure of the program is very personal and can range anywhere from 15 to 30 mins of listening daily and can take anywhere from 10 to 40 weeks to complete the foundational protocol.

Chapter Resources

MOVE TO LEARN

Enabling Every Child To Learn, Move to Learn, www.movetolearn.com.au, info@movetolearning.com.au.

INPP

Introduction to INPP, The Institute For Neuro – Physiological Psychology, wwwinpp.org.uk. *INPP Australia*, Integrating Thinking, www.integratingthinking.com.au/inpp-australia.

BILATERAL INTEGRATION

Ian McGowan, https://uk.linkedin.com/in/ian-mcgowan-b1556721 and ian@mlcscotland.com.

EXTRA LESSON

Extra Lesson Training, The Extra Lesson, www.theextralesson.com.

RMT

Movement-based, Primitive Reflex Integration Program, Rhythmic Movement Training International, www.rhythmicmovement.org.

BRAIN GYM

Brain Gym Australia, www.braingym.org.au.

The Brain Gym Program, Breakthroughs International, www.braingym.org.

LEARNING BREAKTHROUGH

Learning Breakthrough Program, "Think Faster, Focus Better and Remember More For a Happier Life", www.learningbreakthrough.com.

IM

What is Interactive Metronome, Interactive Metronome, www.interactivemetronome.com.

JIAS

Helping Children Achieve, Smart Learning Solutions, www.smartlearning. co.nz/jias-sound-therapy.

Baltic Dyslexia Research Laboratory, Dyslexia Lab, www.dyslexia-lab.dk/.

INTEGRATED LISTENING SYSTEMS (iLs)

iLs Australia, https://aus.integratedlistening.com/.

THE LISTENING PROGRAM

Take the First Step to a Brighter Future, *The Listening Program*, Advanced Brain Technologies, www.advancedbrain.com.

An Insight to Links to Learning, Links to Learning, www.links2learning. com.au.

10

Additional Neurological Support

Working Body

When embarking on neuro-therapies, another area to consider are therapies that assist with having the body in good working order. From experience, I have found the following therapies particularly beneficial as a starting point before other interventions. They may open neurological pathways and the sensory system to assist on the journey of building a bright future!

These therapies are the Neurological Integration System (NIS), osteopathy and massage. I have personally used each of these Allied Health treatments with family and recommend them to clients.

Neurological Integration System (NIS)

NIS is a treatment that allows trained practitioners to understand how and why an individual's brain and body work together a certain way.

Sometimes the body moves away from normal neurological patterns and can get into difficulty as a result. When a qualified practitioner uses NIS as a treatment, they are able to find the basic underlying cause of a complaint, treat it and give their patient effective, long-term relief.

How NIS works

When looking at how NIS works it is important to understand that the body is controlled by the brain and nervous system. A small disruption within the brain and nervous system may make the body not function at its best and become overloaded. During treatment, the NIS practitioner looks for and adjusts what is potentially interfering with the nervous system and the patient's symptoms can be eased.

What issues does NIS address?

NIS treatments may assist with a wide range of conditions. These might be; structural complaints relating to the spine, muscles, tendons, ligaments and joints; immune, digestive and respiratory systems issues; heart related and chronic conditions; be struggling to fight viral, bacterial and fungal infections; or living with stress, depression and anxiety in their everyday lives.

Osteopathy

Osteopathy is a specific treatment which works with the structure and function of the body to assist with maintaining its mechanical function.

For example, any problems with the body's framework may affect someone's health and wellbeing and interrupt the circulatory system and nerves throughout the body. So, osteopaths treat the structure and function of the body, thus helping to increase blood flow throughout the body, assisting an individual in returning to a state of balance and harmony.

What is Cranial Osteopathy?

Cranial osteopathy is a specific type of treatment some osteopaths use to assist with releasing stress and tension throughout the body, particularly in the head.

This treatment is both gentle and effective and may be used across a wide range of people of all ages, from birth to the elderly. It may help babies who are having feeding and sleep disturbances, colic, sickness or wind, as well as children and adults who suffer from recurrent ear infections, asthma, sinus and adenoidal problems. It may also benefit individuals who suffer from learning and behavioural difficulties such as autism, ADD, ADHD, dyslexia, dyspraxia.

Massage

Massage is a controlled hands-on technique whereby a trained therapist applies pressure to the muscles and tissues of the body. A therapist will use different strokes and pressure through the application of different techniques, such as myofascial release and myofascial trigger points to improve joint movement by reducing tension and restoring equilibrium of joint musculature.

Massage may help increase relaxation and reduce stress, as well as being beneficial in assisting rehabilitation after surgery and improving joint mobility and flexibility. Some individuals may find it helpful as a therapy before or after a stressful situation or event.

When the body is in a high state of stress, the level of cortisol rises. Massage can be a great treatment as it relieves tight muscles through increasing blood flow, thus reducing the amount of stress and cortisol, aiding the body in returning to a state of balance.

Some individuals with learning challenges and motor difficulties may find this an effective treatment as it can help them feel more in tune and connected with their body and the world around them. It may also be an effective treatment when used with other therapies and treatments through assisting with improved focus, concentration and tactile sensitivities. Deep, firm pressure through massage may help an individual with challenges to become more alert as a result of their nervous system becoming more relaxed and having greater awareness of their body.

Bean Bag, Ball and Marble Activities

Activities using bean bags, balls and marbles can be a fun and stimulating therapy that supports neurological development.

Bean bag and ball exercises can help develop the function of the right hemisphere of the brain as well as developing greater body awareness by using the senses. They can be a great addition to classrooms to wake up a student's brain while having fun social interaction and releasing any tension or anxiety.

As well as in the classroom, they can be a great addition at home before homework or a sporting activity such as swimming or basketball training or game. The brain likes different textures and sizes so a variety of different sized bean bags — large and small — and textures — bouncy, soft or hard — and shapes is ideal.

Both the sensory and neurological systems can be challenged by increasing the difficulty level once one level is mastered. It is important to remember to begin at a level appropriate to an individual's balance and sensory system development. The levels are detailed first, followed by some suggested exercises.

Pre-Level One

If an individual has difficulty with their balance, bean bag or marble exercises can be done simply by sitting in a chair. This allows for the individual to concentrate on performing the movement without struggling to maintain their balance.

Level One

Perform exercises standing up to engage the balance system, senses and further develop motor coordination.

Level Two

Once exercises/movements have been mastered in the upright position and they appear rhythmical and smooth, another layer can be added to challenge the brain, body and senses. This can be done by either:

- reciting nursery rhymes for young children;
- reciting days of the week, months of the year or counting for primary school age children; or
- tongue twisters; i.e. 'Peter, Piper picked a pack of pickled peppers...' or reciting times tables for older children.

Level Three

Level three can be introduced once level two has been mastered and the individual is able to perform the movement fluently at the same time as using their auditory and visual systems.

While performing the motor task a child can look at the bean bag or ball to further stimulate the visual, proprioceptive and balance systems.

In level three, to increase the difficulty level, an individual can perform the exercise:

- standing on a balance board or a couple of cushions;
- standing on one leg; or
- walking along a balance beam.

Level Four

This last level involves using all the senses at once — tactile, proprioceptive, visual, auditory, vestibular. It is multi-sensory, and the child should be able to perform the task:

- reciting something verbal;
- using your eyes to follow the bean bag/ball; and
- standing on a balance board, cushions, one leg or balance beam.

Fun Physical Bean Bag/Ball Activities

Below are some fun physical exercises to encourage and stimulate the balance and sensory system using bean bags or balls. These can be incorporated with different age groups and these I learnt through the two books after this section and my training with Extra Lesson. I have also included some exercises that have been further developed from some original exercises. These have been individually developed from a group of boys I have gotten to know while working with them over the last two years during basketball training sessions and are listed under 'Sporting Group'.

Age Range: 18–24 months
- Balloon throw and catch using two hands.
- Pass and release beanbag from hand to hand.
- Rolling the ball to each other with two hands while sitting opposite each other.

Age Range: 2–2.5 years
- Jumping over beanbags or pairs of socks in all directions.
- Placing a bean bag on top of head whilst seated, then tipping head forward and dropping it on floor/hands — repeat backwards.
- Bouncing a ball on the floor and catching it with arms open wide while standing upright.

Age Range: 2.5–3 years
- Dropping a bean bag from hand to hand with arms in front of the body.
- Passing a bean bag around the body.
- Leaning forward pass a bean bag from behind the knees in a figure-eight and changing direction.

Age Range: 3–5 years
- Stand on two cushions throwing and catching with a partner.
- Stand on one leg while blowing bubbles.
- Pass bean bag/ball under the leg.

Age Range: 5 years plus
- Pass bean bag/ball under the leg, throw in the air and catch with the opposite hand.
- Balance on one leg, lift the other leg and pass the bean bag or ball under and over the leg for five seconds. You can build up to ten seconds.
- With a partner stand on a balance board or two cushions, throwing and bouncing a ball, one person bouncing the ball to their partner and the other one throwing their ball. Repeat by changing routine.

Sporting Group

- Stand on one leg, then lift the other leg and pass the bean bag/ball under the leg five to ten times whilst balancing.
- Stand on one leg, then lift the other leg and pass the bean bag/ball under the leg and then around the body.
- Throw the bean bag/ball with the right hand behind the back and up over the left shoulder, catching with the left hand. Repeat in the other direction.
- Bend the knees slightly. Hold the bean bag/ball in the right hand, pass and throw it in the front and catch it with your left hand. Repeat with the left hand.
- Lift the right knee and bounce the ball once on the knee and catch it with your left hand. Repeat on the other side. For an extra challenge bounce the ball twice on the knee before catching.

Stimulating Marble Exercises

These fun exercises, which I learnt through my training in Extra Lesson, can release tension in the calf muscles, stimulate the vestibular and bring about a neurological awareness from the head down to the toes. They may also assist with development and improving:

- balance, coordination and motor planning;
- eye-foot coordination;
- sensory input;
- body awareness;
- focus and concentration; and
- strength of muscles in the foot.

I have also found these marble exercises to be a great way to help an individual become more grounded in their body.

Level One

Child sits on a stool or table so that their feet hang above the floor. Place a marble between the big toe and second toe on each foot. Child must wiggle toes to 'pop' marble out. This is done for each space between the remaining toes.

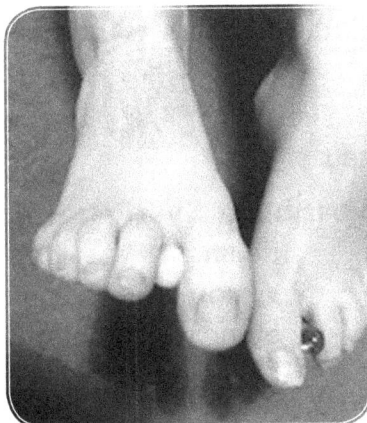

Level Two

Marbles are scattered on the floor. Child then picks up the marbles using their toes, balances and drops them into a basket or box.

Level Three

Marbles are scattered on the floor. Child can pick up marbles using their toes, walk with the marbles in the toes, balance and then drop into a basket or box.

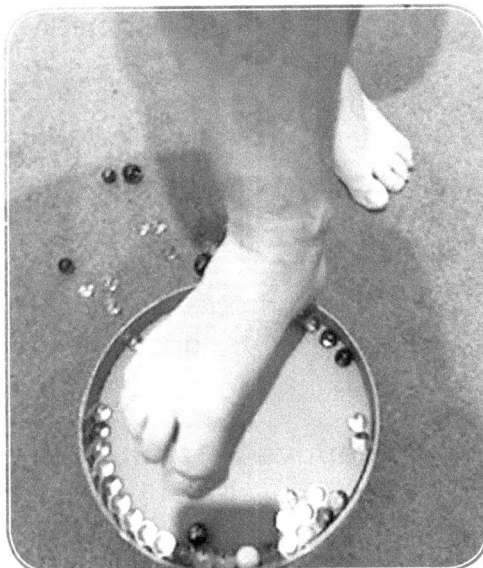

Level Four

This is a variation of Level Three that involves placing a basket or box on a small chair to increase the difficulty. Child then picks up the marbles using their toes, walks with the marbles in the toes, balances and drops it into a basket or box.

Fun activities to stimulate the senses

The following are activities to help stimulate and develop the vestibular and proprioceptive systems, as well as the five senses.

Vestibular System:

- Rolling on the floor in a blanket.
- Windmills — spinning activity.
- Spinning on an office chair.
- Swinging at the park.
- See-Saw at the park.
- Playing row, row, row your boat with a partner — rocking back and forth.
- Rocking in a hammock.
- Rolling forwards and backwards over a large physio ball.
- Jumping and hopping.
- Bouncing up and down on a large physio ball.
- Standing on a balance board.
- Walking over a balance beam.
- Playing games like twister and performing actions to the song *Heads, Shoulders, Knees and Toes*.
- Standing upside down with the feet against the wall.

Proprioceptive System:

- Throwing a bean bag/ball into a basket/container at different distances away.
- Jumping on a trampoline, running and swimming.

- Commando crawling on the stomach.
- Tummy curls.
- Animal walks — bunny hops and frog jumps, etc.
- Wheelbarrow walks.
- Balancing on one leg and catching a ball/bean bag.
- Picking marbles up in the toes.
- Carrying books or boxes.
- Pushing a shopping trolley, gardening and cleaning.

Auditory Sense:

- Sound therapy (Auditory Stimulation).
- Singing, dancing or playing a musical instrument to a rhythm.
- Performing different movement patterns to a clapping rhythm or metronome.
- Speaking into a Toobaloo (a Toobaloo is also known as a whisper phone — when you speak into the device you are able to hear your own voice. It is an inexpensive tool which helps with giving auditory feedback).
- Playing games like Simon Says and Musical Chairs.

Visual Sense:

- Eye warmups from Move to Learn's 'Ten Gems for the Brain'.
- Tracking a bean bag and balloon tapping and catching.
- Popping bubbles in the air.
- Bean bag or ball catching activities with a partner.
- Play a game of Eye Spy.
- Playing with a ribbon stick in a figure eight pattern.
- Juggling and scarf throwing and catching.

Tactile Sense:

- Body massage.
- Singing songs where children name different body parts.
- Playing and exploring with sand, shaving foam and play dough.
- Finger painting.
- Picking marbles up with toes.
- Playing in the mud.
- Rolling a spikey ball over the body and naming the different parts.
- Playing with goo or slime.
- Treasure hunt in a bowl of rice — find and name objects whilst blindfolded.

Taste Sense/Oral Dysfunction:

- Sucking through different straws:
  » Different thicknesses — narrow or wide.
  » Different lengths — long or short.
  » Curly or loopy straws.
  » Sucking through a thick liquid like pureed soup/ fruit or a thick shake.
- Different blowing activities:
  » Blowing up a balloon.
  » Blowing a ping pong ball across a table.
  » Blowing bubbles.
  » Blowing musical instruments, e.g. a harmonica.
- Using an electric toothbrush.
- Practise different facial expressions in front of a mirror.
- Pressing the lips in at the side of the mouth to make a fish face and pretending to be a fish by moving your lips in and out.
- Trying different textured and tasting foods.

Children also love making up their own exercises and sensory activities which can be fun to share with their friends as well as adding an extra layer challenging the brain and further enhancing development.

Recommended Readings

When providing additional neurological support to further enhance development, two books I have read and used with clients are: *Take Time* by Mary Nash-Wortham and Jean Hunt and *Physical Activities for Improving Children's Learning and Behavior* by Billye Ann Cheatum and Allison A. Hammond.

Take Time has lots of movement exercises, particularly fun bean bag ones, for parents/carers, teachers and therapists of children with difficulties in speaking, reading, writing and spelling. These exercises stimulate body awareness and encourage an understanding of orientation in space. They also work on the visual system (hand-eye coordination), the vestibular system, spatial awareness and gross motor skills.

Physical Activities for Improving Children's Learning and Behavior outlines how to identify underlying causes of

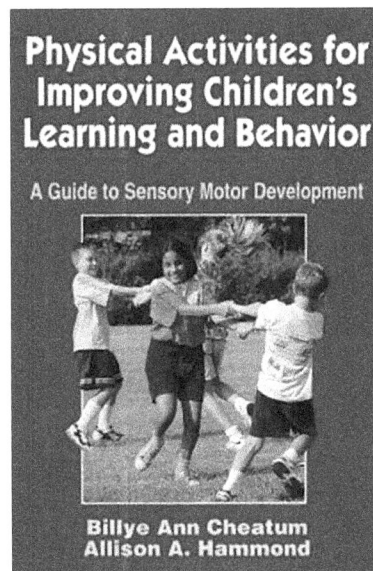

difficulties a child may be having and gives lots of fun motor activities. The authors of this book have worked in the field of special physical education for over 40 years. This book is very easy to understand and includes more than 130 photos of developmental activities to help improve clumsiness, motor coordination and hyperactivity in and out of the classroom.

In summary, the working body interventions and exercises outlined in this chapter may have many benefits with improving an individual's challenges and ultimately help towards building their brightest future. No one treatment is better than the other, and some can be used in conjunction with another, while others can be used by themselves.

Each program takes time and effort, but with consistency and commitment, they may all improve motor coordination, concentration, focus, attention, academics, social well-being, even sports performance. Do some research of your own, find a practitioner and start with a program you think will be engaging and fun for your child, school or centre.

Chapter Resources

NIS

How does NIS work?, Neuro Link, neurolinkglobal.com/what-is-nis/how-does-nis-work/. *Neurological Based Health Care*, Dr Bianca Dobson, https://www.drbiancadobson.com.au/.

NIS — Neurological Integration System, Body Link, https://www.bodylink.co.nz/services/what-is-nis/.

OSTEOPATHS

Osteopathy, Family Wellness Group, Encore Health, http://familywellnessgroup.com.au/services/osteopathy/.

Osteopathy, Geoffrey Fong Osteopathic Services Camberwell, https://www.fong.com.au/osteopathy/.

MASSAGES

Massage Therapy, Encyclopedia of Children's Health, healthofchildren.com/M/Massage-Therapy.html.

Massage in Learning Difficulties: physio.co.uk, physio.co.uk/treatments/massage/massage-for-client-groups/massage-in-learning-difficulties.php, sensory-processing-disorder.com/massage-therapy-for-spd.html.

Massage for pain and movement, Celebral Palsy Alliance, cerebralpalsy.org.au/our-research/about-cerebral-palsy/interventions-and-therapies/massage-for-pain-and-movement/.

Welcome to City Haven Massage, https://cityhavenmassage.com.au/

BEAN BAG AND MARBLE LEVELS

Extra Lesson Training, The Extra Lesson, www.theextralesson.com.

Audrey E. McAllen, 2004, *The Extra Lesson*, page 103, Rudolf Steiner College Press.

Mary Nash-Wortham & Jean Hunt, 2003, *Take Time*, pages 48 – 60, The Robinswood Press.

ACTIVITIES TO STIMULATE SYSTEMS AND SENSES

Billye Ann Cheatum and Allison A. Hammond, 2000, *Physical Activities for Improving Children's Learning and Behaviour*, pages 251–255, 295, 325–327, Human Kinetics.

School-age Vision: 6 to 18 years, American Optometric Association, www.aoa.org/patients-and-public/good-vision-throughout-life/childrens-vision/school-aged-vision-6-to-18-years-of-age.

The Gustatory System, SPD Australia, www.spdaustralia.com.au/the-gustatory-system/. *Saliva Control in Children*, The Royal Children's Hospital Melbourne, www.rch.org.au/uploadedFiles/Main/Content/plastic/salivabook.pdf.

BOOK REFERENCES

Mary Nash-Wortham & Jean Hunt, 2003, *Take Time*, The Robinswood Press.

Billye Ann Cheatum and Allison A. Hammond, 2000, *Physical Activities for Improving Children's Learning and Behavior*, Human Kinetics.

BRIGHT FUTURES
TESTIMONIALS

Stories and Testimonials

Lisa and Stuart, parents of 13-year-old boy in Educational Moves and tutoring everyday (from Chapter 7 — The Plastic Brain)

"Our son had a challenging start to his year seven year, being quite overwhelmed with the demands of a big high school. We decided home schooling was the best way for him to get his confidence back. We found Educational Moves and began working tutoring sessions with Mark on a one-on-one basis a week for English and Maths. The rapport Mark built with our son enabled him to start having a go and believing in himself again.

"It wasn't long before Mark was working everyday with him and he was coping with the workload. Mark developed a structured timetable for our son to add geography, science, music, art, history and a language to his everyday schedule. Our son has achieved excellent results in his subjects and developed confidence in his ability to learn with Mark. In his words, "this is easy!"

"Mark and home tutoring on a daily basis over six months enabled us to transition our son back into school for the next year.

"We are so happy, not just with his academic success but his newfound confidence and belief within himself."

Kerrie, Mother of 14-year-old girl in Extra Lesson

"My daughter was diagnosed with 'global delays' at about two. Since then our daughter has improved physically. She is much more coordinated now and is currently having dance lessons which before she couldn't do – thanks to our journey to find the best support for her.

"One of the most effective therapies we have found is the Movement Program. Cognitively, her reading, writing and understanding have improved greatly, she can now read the newspaper.

"It takes commitment from both parent and child, but it's not an unreasonable amount of time considering the excellent results!"

Claire, Mother of 8-year-old girl in Move to Learn

"I was recommended to see Jenny by a work colleague after talking about some of the difficulties my child was having at school. Jenny was lovely and welcoming to my anxious child and instantly created a connection with her.

"As a result of the Move to Learn exercises undertaken with Jenny, my daughter improved her motor skills and balance, which I believe assisted her confidence and her learning at school."

Melissa and John, Parents of 7-year-old boy in Move to Learn and JIAS Listening Therapy

"Our son was originally diagnosed with apraxia and had been using speech therapy for quite a while without making much progress.

"We knew that there was more to his challenges than just apraxia and started searching for someone. Thankfully we found Jenny and started working with her to address his underlying issues with brain integration.

"The improvements we saw through movement and sound therapy were wonderful, and in a very short time he started to make improvements in all areas (fine and gross motor skills, auditory and speech skills) and he continues to do so."

Liz, Mother of 13-year-old boy in JIAS Listening Therapy

"JIAS Listening Therapy with Jenny has been amazing! Our son, now 13 has autism, intellectual delay and dyslexia. At the beginning of the therapy he had a huge delay in processing language. You would ask him a question or instruction and wait for an answer/response. Often times there was none as it was just too difficult.

"Now you can give him a set of complex instructions and he responds in seconds. He is also more verbal with greater eye contact. What's more, he has enjoyed it and now loves a wide range of music. We travelled three hours each way for the appointments and it was well worth it. Jenny has a wealth of knowledge and personal experience. I would recommend it to anyone with autism or language processing difficulties."

Diane, Mother of 11-year-old boy in INPP Movement Program

"Before commencing the INPP program, my son was very social and competent at sport. His main challenges were working independently in class, as well as finding maths, spelling, reading and writing challenging. He also suffered frequent headaches and tiredness at the end of each school day.

"After approximately 12 months doing the INPP movement program his sporting skills excelled and the headaches and tiredness he had suffered from reduced by 75 per cent. Academically he became less reliant on an Integration Aide in the classroom and his maths, spelling, reading and writing improved."

The graph below shows his overall improvement in his assessment of primitive and postural reflexes.

The numbers up the side of the graph represent a score out of four during the initial and post assessments with regards to primitive and postural reflexes — a score of four indicates a strong presence of a primitive reflex and under-developed postural reflex.

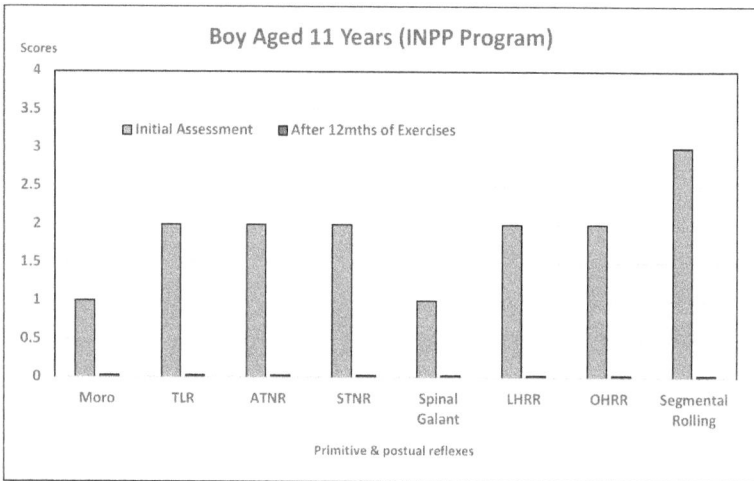

Boy Aged 11 Years (INPP Program)

THE TANSLEY STANDARD VISUAL FIGURES TEST (A.E. TANSLEY, 1967) – A STANDARD TEST FOR VISUAL-PERCEPTION.

Initial Assessment

THE TANSLEY STANDARD VISUAL FIGURES TEST (A.E. Tansley, 1967)

Assessment – after twelve months on INPP

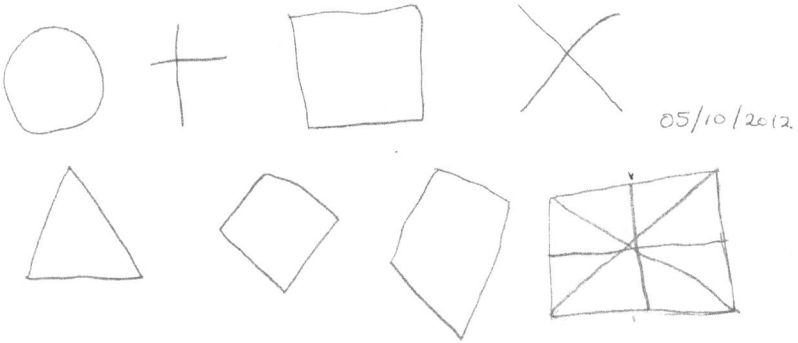

05/10/2012

DRAW A PERSON TEST

Initial Assessment

Assessment – after twelve months on INPP Program

05/10/2012

21/07/11

Diane, Mother of 11-year-old boy in JIAS Sound Therapy

"Before JIAS my son had completed 10 months on the INPP Movement Program. He still showed some challenges with his comprehension, confusion with speech sounds and difficulty remembering instructions. He lacked confidence when reading and was sensitive to some sounds and certain teacher's voices.

"After 12 weeks of JIAS Sound Therapy he showed improvement in his reading, he was much more talkative, and was able to decode sounds better, particularly the 'R' sound. He was much more confident through being able to better understand and remember instructions."

Danielle, Mother of 6-year-old boy in Move to Learn

"Discovering Jenny's service has made a difference to my son's entire life. In the short-term it was just helping him join a line at school, enabling him to have spatial awareness and not touch other children.

"Four years on it has meant he is a well-adjusted child who has many friends and is not looked on as the 'naughty' child who can't sit still and is disruptive. We will be forever grateful to Jenny and her wonderful, kind approach that supports children, regardless of their busy, crazy personalities!"

Judy, Mother of 7-year-old boy and his 5-year-old-brother in The Listening Program

"My oldest son was very troubled and after being told by my GP to find some alternative therapy for him, as mainstream medicine was not going to improve his problems, I found The Listening Program and he started on it within a couple of months.

"The improvement in his behaviour was fantastic. He has gone from a child who didn't want to engage with people to one who is now cheeky and does engage. So, when his younger brother started to show similar problems in reception, I had him tested and he started The Listening Program with Tracey from Links to Learning. He went from an average student to one that was top of his class. His teacher who had said to me that I was wasting my money had to admit she was wrong and how surprised she is with the results that we have achieved.

"The Listening program has improved our family life immensely and I would recommend it. I now say life is better with music."

Sarah, Mother of 5-year-old boy in The Listening Program

"I originally sought support from Tracey at Links to Learning for concerns I had over my son's challenges. My son was a bright and intelligent young person but appeared to be highly sensitive and he found it challenging to follow instructions. Quite often he needed instructions repeated and he had difficulty understanding what was being said in a group situation.

"At the initial appointment my son showed poor eye contact and he heavily resisted having headphones on his head. This initial testing showed he was on the first percentile but finally I was relieved that I had some reasons as to why he didn't answer when spoken to, couldn't keep up in conversations and felt overwhelmed by the world at large.

"My son resisted the program at the start, but perseverance won out and we started to see improvements. We saw less meltdowns and it appeared he was feeling less overwhelmed and he was also getting better at following instructions.

"From continuing to work with Tracey his ability to catch, run, and adapt to quick movements, plus his willingness to jump, climb and tumble increased. Anything that stimulated his vestibular system was highly triggering for him, but he slowly became more willing to tolerate being off balance.

"My son now enjoyed jumping on a trampoline, something which he avoided before starting the program. He gained confidence when moving his body and was much more aware of where he was in the world.

"His teacher noticed that his ability to concentrate in a noisy classroom was significantly improving as well as his overall confidence. By the end of 2019, his second year at school, his teacher was commenting that she could now clearly hear his voice over his peers when they were calling out answers.

"At home we noticed an improvement in his eye contact and that he was able to hear us when we called out from another room. We can have conversations in busy shopping centres or out and about walking side by side. His confidence has soared, he speaks up for himself, shows off his enormous personality, and after initial introductions will chat with people.

"He began struggling with his reading and phonics but through continued integration and listening program support, jumped from being one of the lowest level readers to the third highest reading level in his class and the highest reader level of the boys in his year.

"We have seen incredible brain maturation through the continued use of The Listening Program. His ability to explain his thoughts and concepts has improved dramatically, and he now easily physically and socially interacts in his world.

"We are incredibly grateful and appreciative for finding this program and Tracey's expertise, understanding, and guidance through Aidan's journey. Finally, people are seeing the amazing young man that we know he is!"

Tabitha*, Mother of 6-year-old girl in JIAS Sound Therapy

"My daughter has recently completed the Johansen Individualised Auditory Stimulation Programme (JIAS) through Glynis Brummer at Smart Learning Solutions. To say we are blown away by the results is simply not enough, it truly has changed my daughter's life.

"When my daughter started school, it became clear that she was struggling. She was exhausted and emotionally worn. Teacher feedback was that she had difficulty following instructions, was easily distracted and her spelling and reading was below expectation. As a result, her confidence was rock bottom. At this time, we were referred to Glynis for JIAS treatment.

"At the end of the initial assessment, it was immediately clear my daughter had very low sensitivity in both ears to hearing higher frequencies required for language. She was sitting far below the optimum listening curve, so discriminating and perceiving language sounds was difficult. Being more sensitive to low frequency ranges meant that she was easily overpowered by environmental (i.e. classroom) noises and disturbances. In addition to this, crossovers were occurring which means what information she did hear was poorly processed and much of it was lost.

"We immediately began JIAS treatment aimed at minimising the sensitivity in the lower frequencies and increasing sensitivity in the higher frequencies through listening to specialised music. Her progress was incredible and soon evident to her teacher, who began to remark on her improvements in her school work and her confidence. She was more and more able to process language, information and instructions correctly. As her teacher now puts it, "she is like a different kid all together". She is no longer dreading school or feeling incapable. Her learning and school grades have improved drastically. A weight has been lifted and she is so happy. Thank you, Glynis!"

Natalie*, 15-year-old girl in INPP Program

"I am writing to you about treatment I received from you four or five years ago. I had really bad physiological reactions to travel and being away from the controlled everyday environment. The physiological response to these situations was very crippling for me growing up. I couldn't go anywhere without it causing major anxiety, continuous vomiting and psychological distress that was taxing on my body and mind.

"My parents heard about your practice and after years of struggling with these issues I came to see you for remedial treatment. I cannot explain how much your treatment helped me! We had tried so many different solutions to the problem I was struggling with. I always hoped that one of them would be the one that just clicked yet they didn't.

"All it took was two sessions with you and then repeated practicing of the exercises you gave me for it to make a difference. Your treatment changed my life. I am now able to travel and explore without severe anxiety and stress responses. I have been to many countries since seeing you, including travelling to Nepal by myself for a month. This would not have happened without your help. You had such a positive impact on my life, and I am so thankful for that. Thank you, Glynis from Smart Learning Solutions."

About the Author

As a mother of three boys and Director of Educational Moves, I have over 30 years of experience in fitness, swim teaching, neuro development movement and sound therapy.

My interest in Developmental Movement and Sound Therapy arose from its success in helping two of my children improve their learning, focus and concentration, motor coordination, sports performance and social engagement.

I have completed training in: Move to Learn; INPP (Institute for Neuro-Physiological Psychology Method); Bilateral Integration; Extra Lesson; Rhythmic Movement; Johansen Individualised Auditory Stimulation (JIAS); Integrated Listening Systems (iLs); and The Listening Program (TLP).

From my training, I have experience designing and supervising home-based programs for my own children plus many others. I have also personally organised and presented seminars/workshops in the Move to Learn program for parents, educators and many allied health professionals.

As well as this, I have organised and coordinated international training for two colleagues in Melbourne, Ian McGowan, from the Movement and Learning Centre in Scotland, and Glynis Brummer, from Smart Learning Solutions in Auckland, New Zealand.

Ian has travelled to Melbourne and presented several training courses in Bilateral Integration and Glynis has delivered many four-day training sessions in Johansen Individualised Auditory Stimulation.

All of this experience has provided me with a unique insight into the needs of children, their parents and the support they both require to achieve a high level of life skills for their child.

Experience as an organiser, presenter and speaker

Organiser

Over the last ten years I have organised and coordinated many professional development workshops for two international presenters to deliver training in Melbourne on JIAS Sound Therapy and Bilateral Integration. Glynis Brummer from Smart Learning Solutions in Auckland, New Zealand has presented several JIAS Sound Therapy courses, and Ian McGowan from the Movement and Learning Centre in Scotland has delivered training in Bilateral Integration. Attendees at these workshops have been early childhood educators, teachers, Allied Health professionals, PE teachers and sports coaches.

Presenter and Speaker

As a presenter and speaker over the last eight years I have organised and presented professional development workshops and information seminars in:

- Move to Learn Workshop:
  » Full day for Educators and Allied Health Professionals
  » Three-hour parent workshop.
- Learning strategies – primitive and postural reflexes.
- Fun bean bag and ball exercises for focus and concentration.
- Sports performance — exercises to enhance athletic performance.

Through organising international training and my knowledge in the area of neuro-development movement and sound therapies, I have become an experienced and passionate presenter. Personally, this is in the area of the Move to Learn program and other neuro-therapy topics and is noted from individuals who have attended some of my workshops/seminars.

Workshop/Seminar Feedback

"I feel extremely privileged to attend Jenny's workshops and receive her training. Her calling to share her personal and professional experience and knowledge is a true inspiration that has benefited the lives of many.

I found her workshops extremely valuable, informative and practical, presented in her professional and nurturing passionate style. I highly recommend."

– Sandra

"I have attended a Move to Learn Workshop presented by Jenny and found that she is very knowledgeable about this subject, and she presents it in a way that is respectful of all attendees.

She is very approachable, organised and willing to answer questions both on the day and afterwards. As an early childhood educator in a preschool, Jenny enabled me to bring this knowledge that would normally be taught on a one-on-one basis and adapt it to our service for the benefit of all children."

– Vicki
Director/Nominated Supervisor at Coleambally Preschool

"I thoroughly enjoyed attending workshops presented by Jenny. Her knowledge on the brain-body connection in regards to learning and wellbeing has enhanced the way I work in my own practice.

Jenny presents with passion based on real life experiences and has a natural down to earth manner.

Building Bright Futures is her latest achievement that explains the building blocks to achieving a better tomorrow."

– Jayne
Neurodevelopmental Therapist at www.dyslexiamelbourne.com

"My first encounter with Jenny was when I signed up for my first Move to Learn workshop as an eager parent searching for real solutions to my children's learning difficulties. Jenny was very helpful, supportive and went the extra mile to accommodate all my questions and concerns.

Doing her workshop was a life changing experience for me and my family. I decided to become a practitioner, and I left there feeling so empowered and equipped to be able to help my children and begin a new line of work after being a stay at home mum for so many years. I believe a big part of that decision was Jenny. She is an amazing educator and mentor, who really knows what she is talking about. Her gentle, down-to-earth approach makes her relatable, and she has an ability to connect with where individuals and their family's needs are really at.

She has a profound skill to teach and break down a complex subject so well, making it easy to understand, teach, implement and apply right away, which reflects years of personal and professional experience. Her passion and purpose is so evident, you can't help but see this from the moment you meet Jenny. Her heart is to support children, parents and their families the best way she can and whatever means possible, always going above and beyond, putting so much of herself into overdelivering, amazing value.

It has been a true blessing to be taught this modality from Jenny of Educational Moves. She gave me the confidence to help and support my family's developmental needs through this modality. Eventually I started my own business called Nurosteps as a neuro-motor developmental educator and sound therapy practitioner, which has been very successful for five years, helping and supporting families in the same way. I am no longer practising in this field but I am helping others shine through my community-based practice 'Let Light In You'. Thank you Jenny for all you are and especially the great work you continue to do."

– Jennifer

Acknowledgements

I t is with much gratitude that I would like to express how grateful I am to my friend and colleague Ian McGowan in taking the time to write a *Foreword* for my book. Thank you!

Utmost thanks to Helen Hatherly for writing a special note for my book during her busy time as a Principal. I really appreciate it!

I am so thankful to Sandra Garvey for all her support, creativity and management of the artwork for this book. Also, for her contribution to the title — amazing work!

Special thanks to a dear friend of mine whose daughter kindly provided me with the developmental photos of her child, I am so grateful!

I am also thankful to all of the Movement and Listening Neuro Therapy organisations for their permission to give a brief description of what their programs are about is outlined in Chapter 9.

A very special thank you to Vanessa Nicoletti age 10 for her hand drawn illustrations on pages 60 and 86.

Thank you to the Urban Child Institute for giving me permission to use their graphic image of 'Synapse Density Over Time' depicted in Chapter 5.

I am so thankful for Glynis Brummer from Smart Learning Solutions in New Zealand for kindly providing two stories from families she has worked with.

Special thanks to Tracey Butler from Links to Learning in Adelaide for providing some stories of two families she has worked with.

I am so thankful to all the families I have worked with over the years and other Developmental Movement and Sound Therapy practitioners with whom I have made wonderful friendships.

Special thanks to some of the families I have worked with for providing their child's story of achievement depicted in Stories and Testimonials.

Lastly, thank you to Charlotte Long and everyone at Busybird Publishing for your management, expert advice, guidance and support in editing and publishing this book.

www.ingramcontent.com/pod-product-compliance
Lightning Source LLC
Chambersburg PA
CBHW060234030426

42335CB00014B/1444